CREATIVE AD DESIGN & ILLUSTRATION

FRESH AS SPRING
HEINZ
Tomato and Onio
SPREAD
HEINZ
Sandwich
SPREAD
WAKE UP!
TIRED & ASLEEP
DAVID JUNIPER

CREATIVE AD DESIGN & ILLUSTRATION

DICK WARD

NORTH LIGHT BOOKS

Cincinnati, Ohio

© Macdonald & Co (Publishers) Ltd 1988
© Text Dick Ward Airways Ltd. 1988

First published in Great Britain in 1988 by
Macdonald & Co (Publishers) Ltd
London & Sydney

A Pergamon Press plc company

First published in North America
in 1988 by North Light Books, an imprint of
F & W Publications, Inc.,
1507 Dana Ave.,
Cincinnati, Ohio 45207

All rights reserved
No part of this publication may be
reproduced, stored in a retrieval system, or
transmitted, in any form or by any means
without the prior permission in writing of the
publisher, nor be otherwise circulated in any
form of binding or cover other than that in
which it is published and without a similar
condition including this condition being
imposed on the subsequent purchaser.

Printed and bound in Italy by OFSA SpA
ISBN 0-89134-244-3

CONTENTS

INTRODUCTION	6
1 AIRBRUSH	8
2 ACRYLIC	32
3 WATERCOLOUR	56
4 LINE AND WASH	72
5 PENCIL	86
6 SCRAPERBOARD (SCRATCHBOARD)	108
7 CARTOON	120
8 PHOTO-MONTAGE	130
9 COMPUTERS	142
INDEX	157

Free banking for the OVER 60's

As well as offering a full range of banking services, the over 60's can now enjoy free banking! See our free leaflet for details.

TSB BANK

THE BANK THAT LIKES TO SAY YES.

INTRODUCTION

The aim of this book is to show the skills and amount of creative thinking that goes into producing a modern advertising illustration. As many different styles of artwork as possible have been used to give an idea of the range of techniques involved in advertising work. The roles of the client, the advertising agency, the art director and the copywriter are all discussed. The stress, however, is on the role of the artist in the process and the methods that he/she uses to create the effects required by the brief.

The client sets the tone of the campaign by asking for an 'image' of the product to be conveyed in a particular way. The client will know what type of people the campaign is trying to reach; the position of the product in the market and how much money is to be spent.

Once all these factors have been taken into account and a brief has come from the client, then the art director can begin to make decisions about how to communicate the product's image. Sometimes the copy comes first and the visual image has to support it, but in other cases the illustration or photograph is the first part. Often the type of ad limits the choice of technique: for instance, with a newspaper campaign scraperboard (scratchboard) may be a wise choice because it reproduces extremely well in black and white. A major campaign with vast media coverage, including posters and press ads in quality magazines, opens up many more possibilities. Whatever technique is chosen the finished ad must convey the image of the product that the client wants. No matter how good the illustration is, if it fails to enhance the profile of the product then it has failed to do its job.

The artist is only a small part of the campaign, even though the illustration may be the main part of the ad. Many illustrators, especially newcomers to the business, forget that they are just one of a large team. Advertising is a tough profession and artists doing commercial work need both skill and stamina to survive. They have to work to strict deadlines: no newspaper or magazine is going to wait for the work to be finished, even if it is one of exceptionally high quality. At stake in every campaign are the reputations of the client, its product, the agency and a great deal of money.

It is remarkable how many people forget that an artist has to start with a blank piece of paper. Images do not appear by magic – someone has to draw or paint them. Furthermore, the artist has to make a living from his work. It is still regarded as fun – which of course it can be – but not necessarily at three o'clock in the morning, with a 9 am deadline approaching and a disaster on your drawing board!

All the campaigns featured in this book presented difficult creative problems which have been resolved effectively. At the time of writing it is too early to judge the success of all of them, but the campaign for Wines from Spain has helped sales to rise by over 30 per cent.

The use of free pencil illustration in the campaign for the Dunkerque Tourist Board solved the creative problem of conveying a romantic and picturesque image for the town. A tighter pencil style was chosen by the art director of the Kleenex campaign. Here, the artist had to suggest softness and gentleness to reflect the qualities of the product.

With the campaign for Evian the art director decided to use an artist who had never worked in watercolour before. This imaginative decision was rewarded by the fresh, spontaneous nature of her illustrations which reflect the product's image extremely well.

British Rail began their campaign with a radio ad similar in style to a 1950s science-fiction series. This was followed up with a series of visual ads, based on a similar theme. The technique used – photo-montage – is an unusual one, but is very well suited to capture the flavour of 1950s science-fiction magazines.

Two campaigns showing the use of acrylic painting are illustrated. For Bell's Whisky the idea was to make the illustration look like a genuine old master canvas to emphasize the quality of the product. The photocopier manufacturers, Océ, wanted the quality of the illustration on their brochure to reflect the quality of their product and to tempt potential customers to order a print.

To promote Barclays Bank's Connect Card, a new idea in organizing personal finance, it was decided that the illustration style should reflect the technology of the card and explain its use very clearly. Airbrush was also used in the Borg-Warner Chemicals campaign to present the product in a more attractive and eye-catching way.

Advertising illustration has often been regarded as a substitute for photography or as a cheaper alternative. I hope these pages will show that creative art directors are realizing how many options illustration opens and how effective it can be in putting across the advertiser's message.

Dick Ward

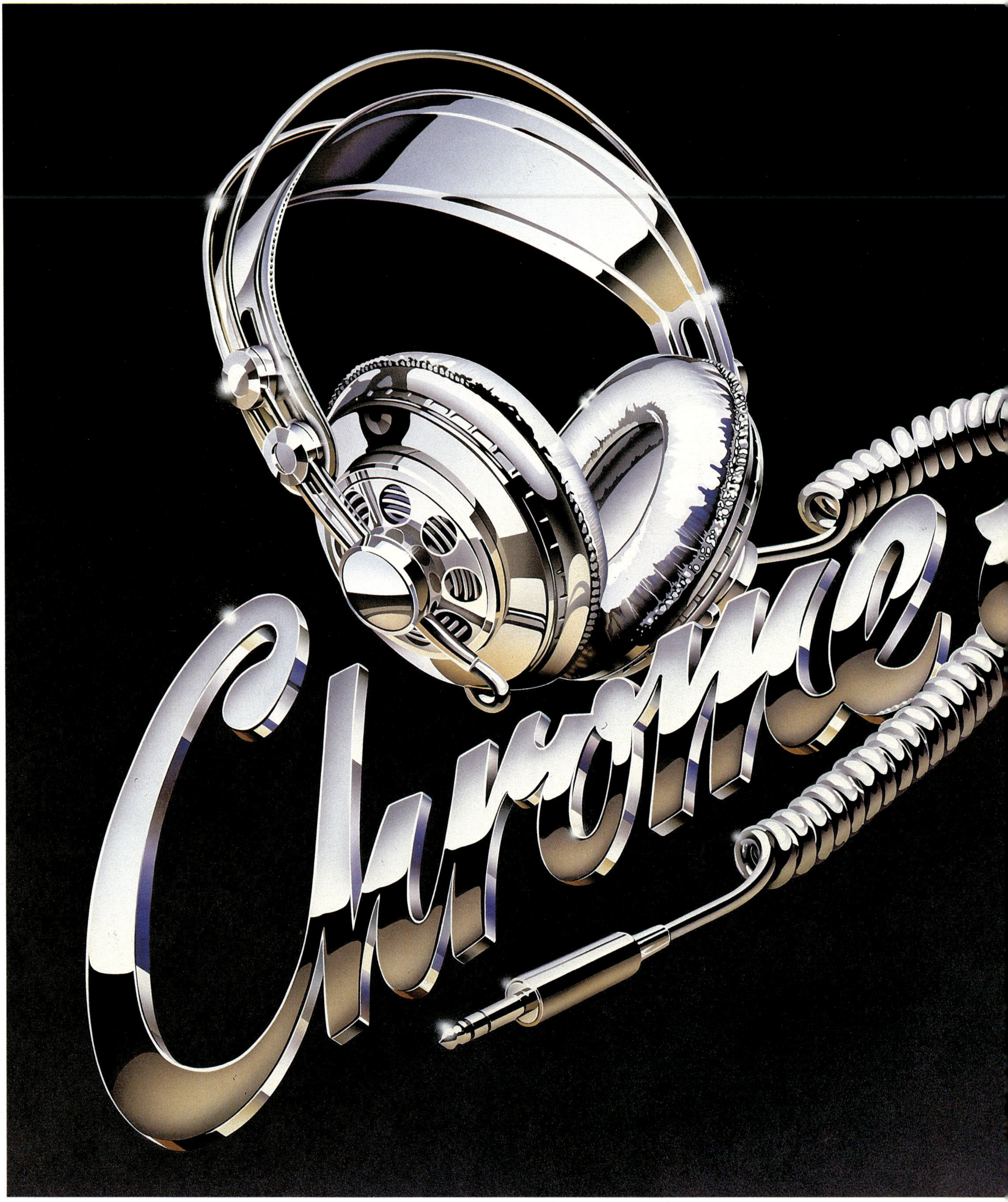
Chrome

AIRBRUSH

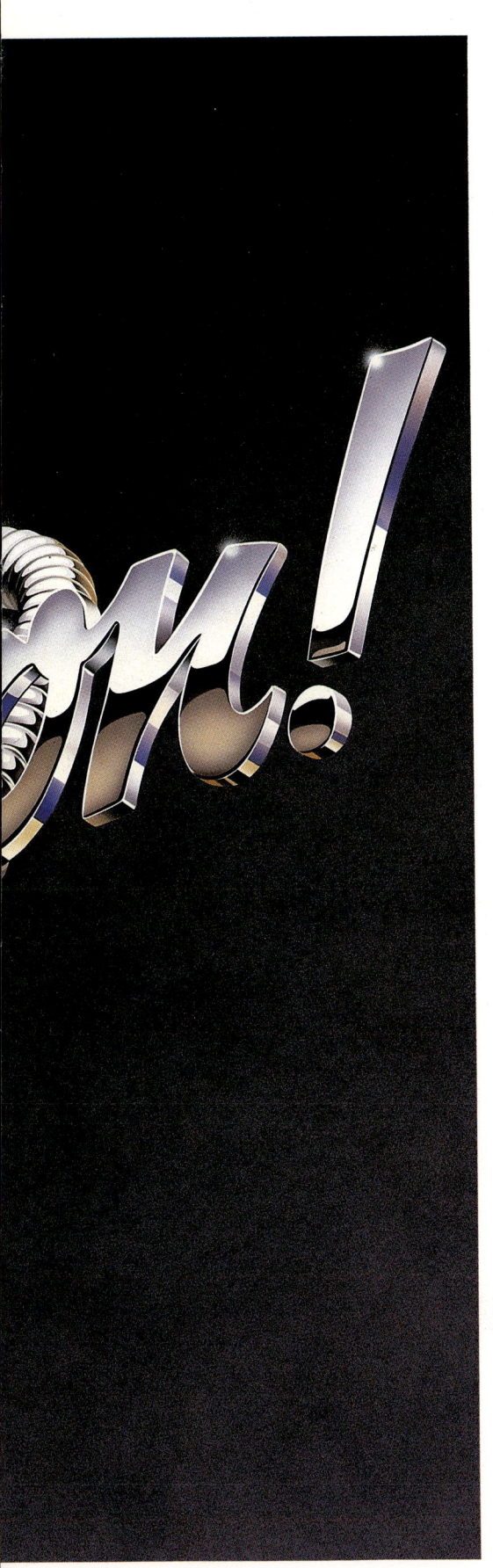

The airbrush was invented in the latter part of the nineteenth century and was used mainly for retouching. The principle on which the airbrush works is very simple: air flows into the brush forcing paint to be expelled in a fine spray. It wasn't until the 1930s that its potential as an illustrative instrument was fully realized, and even then, its use was confined to technical and industrial work. The airbrush is a highly versatile tool, however, and more adventurous uses and techniques are constantly being developed. The heyday of purist airbrushing was in the 1960s, when artists used an all-encompassing technique, with every segment of the drawing airbrushed. Today, methods are far more varied, with artists using the airbrush combined with other illustrative techniques. Highlights may be scratched in with a scalpel (utility knife) or a typist's eraser may be used, or whole areas may be painted by hand and then merely finished off with the airbrush. So the ability to use an airbrush effectively is an important skill for any illustrator to acquire.

Airbrush illustration by John Harewood for BASF Tapes.

BARCLAYS BANK/THE CLIENT BRIEF

THE CLIENT BARCLAYS BANK
THE BRIEF TO CREATE A POSTER AND POINT OF SALE CAMPAIGN TO LAUNCH BARCLAYS CONNECT CARD – A NEW SYSTEM OF CASH-LESS SHOPPING
THE AGENCY LINTAS
ART DIRECTOR BRIAN CONNOLLY
COPYWRITER JONATHAN ELEY
THE ARTIST PAUL ALLEN

Barclays Connect is a plastic card that can be used as a credit card and at a cash dispenser to draw cash, at home and abroad. It differs from other credit cards in that the user's current bank account is debited directly as and when the card is used. So all transactions are conducted electronically, unlike most other paper-based systems that involve actually sending a piece of paper back to the main clearing banks for every transaction.

Bearing the product in mind, the art director had to choose an illustrative style that conveyed the flexibility and technology of the card in a clear-cut and up-to-the-minute way. An airbrush style seemed particularly suitable for this and Paul Allen has a reputation for using airbrush in a very imaginative way. He is a creative illustrator who gives a great deal of thought to the design of his work. The resulting series of ads look very slick, and suggest that this is the easy way to manage your money. Perhaps the only other approach to this very contemporary campaign would have been computer-generated material.

Interview with Brian Connolly

DICK WARD What was your brief?
BRIAN CONNOLLY We had to produce five posters to launch the Connect Card so

ABOVE **The art director's rough. The artist made the hand more dominant in the final artwork.**

I wanted a style that was quite fresh but at the same time suggested technology.
DW Had Barclays used a lot of illustration in previous campaigns?
BC Yes, in a cross-section of contemporary styles, especially on leaflets. We wanted a style that looked

RIGHT **The finished image which is used as a poster (billboard) and as the front cover of Barclays' point-of-sale leaflet – it has a very contemporary feel.**

very modern and could explain the product clearly.
DW Did you produce the first concepts?
BC Yes. We spent quite a long time discussing what we wanted to say, and how to say it.
DW Why did you choose airbrush.

BARCLAYS BANK/THE CLIENT BRIEF

For details and an application form, pick up this leaflet.

Published by Barclays Bank PLC. Marketing Department. Reg. No. 1026167. Reg. Office: 54 Lombard Street, London EC3P 3AH.

BARCLAYS BANK/THE CLIENT BRIEF

BC We wanted illustrations that were realistic, and also graphic. Many people think airbrushing is old-fashioned, but Paul Allen's style suggests 'hi-tech' and he can draw a hyper-real airbrush image as well. But he's not just an airbrush illustrator: he also has a lot of design ability and uses bold, vibrant colours.
DW What was the purpose of the posters?
BC To show all the functions of the card – so each illustration had to contain strong imagery. There were five elements to show in four posters: you can use it like a credit card, to get cash out, to order things over the telephone and to pay bills in the bank, as well as using it abroad.
DW Can't you do that with any credit card?
BC Yes, but with this card your bank account is debited automatically, unlike an ordinary credit card. So we had to make that clear and easily understood.
DW Was it your idea to incorporate all the graphic devices such as the dot, triangles and arrows?
BC Paul and I worked on it together. The main theme is the hand with the card, and then we chose images that tell a story.
DW How did you hear of Paul?
BC We noticed his work in one of the illustration books. There was a lot going on in each of his drawings, so he was a natural choice.
DW What was your timing on the whole campaign?
BC We finished the posters and leaflets in about two or three months.
DW How many illustrations did that include?
BC There were four quite detailed illustrations for the posters, plus two that were mainly copy and some point-of-sale material.
DW Did you check the traces before going ahead?
BC We kept liaising with Paul all the time, but the basic idea didn't change, although we changed some of the traces around as one had too much imagery in it and another not enough.
DW Do you like an illustrator to have a lot of creative input?
BC Yes. Although I had the basic idea, Paul made a lot of suggestions to add to it, and as far as the colours go, he had a free hand, more or less. I would have been too conservative if I'd chosen the colours – I would never have had cream and purple pyramids with a flat green palm tree, or a blue suitcase with a ruled grid across it! So his input was substantial.
DW Do you think you have more control with illustration as opposed to photography?
BC It's a mixture. With illustration the process is continuous: the illustrator's trace or a layout can be changed at various stages, but with photography you have much less time – you're there on the day and it has to be done there and then.

For the art director's travel poster, the artist made several adjustments to the rough. He enlarged the hand, changed the angle of the suitcase and gave the pyramids a graphic treatment for the final image.

BARCLAYS BANK/THE ARTIST

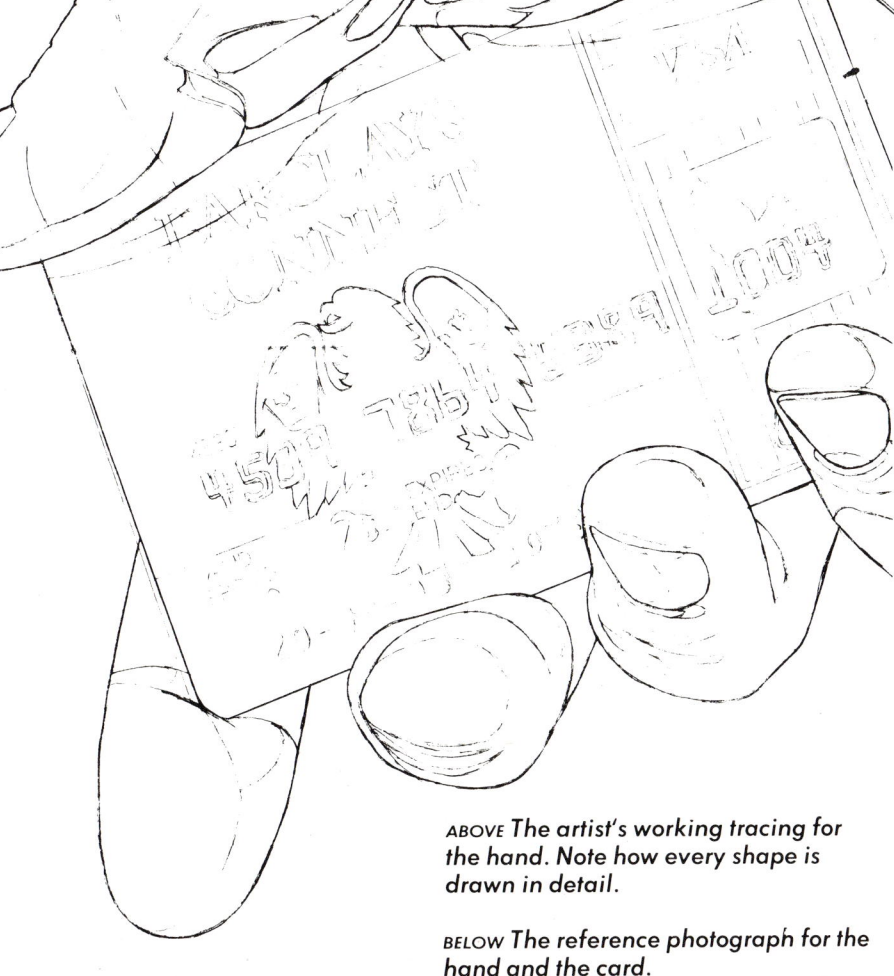

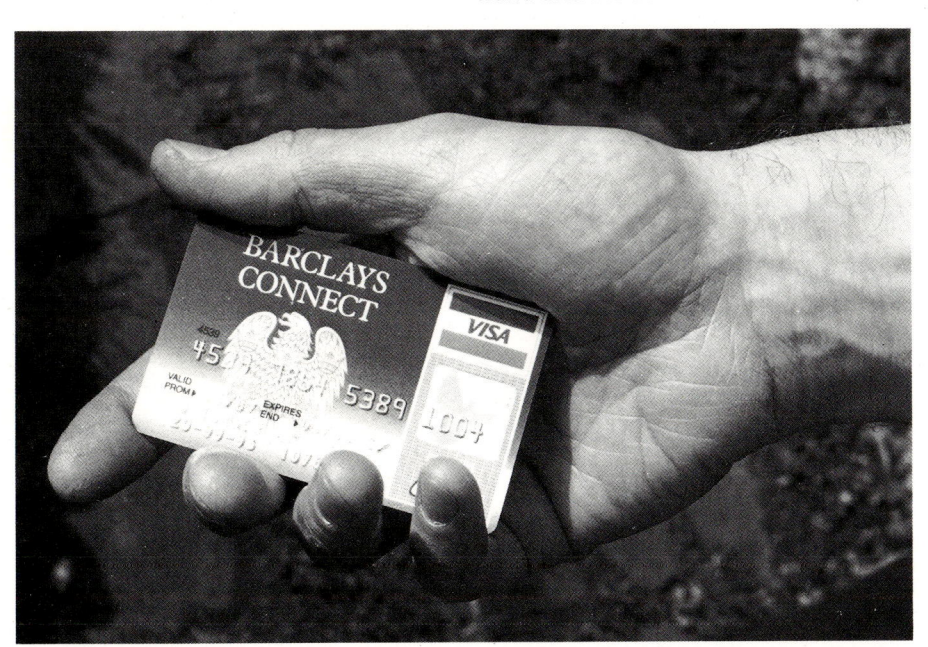

ABOVE **The artist's working tracing for the hand. Note how every shape is drawn in detail.**

BELOW **The reference photograph for the hand and the card.**

Interview with Paul Allen

DICK WARD What was your initial brief?

PAUL ALLEN The art director gave me a visual which I adapted so that it worked.

DW You have made the hand more dominant, compared with the first roughs.

PA Yes. I think the hand is one of the most important elements – the first rough had too much empty space in it – so I enlarged the hand and altered the proportions of the other images to fill the area more comfortably.

DW How do you plan your drawings?

PA I plan each one out in my head first of all, and then find the reference. When I've got all the elements assembled I do accurate traces of the individual pieces, enlarge or reduce them as necessary, to design the whole image.

DW Then you use a copyscanner (Camera Lucida)?

PA Yes. I put all the traces together and do a photocopy of them combined. That goes to the client for approval before I start work.

DW Do you trace down in the normal way?

PA No. I use tracing-down paper, but I trace the image down on top of the adhesive masking film so that I don't mark the board.

DW Do you mask out the outside edge of the drawing?

PA Yes. I like to see the finished image building up – I don't like waiting until the end.

DW Hands are very difficult to draw. How do you go about it?

PA I take very tight detailed black and white photographs.

DW Why do you prefer black and white?

PA It's better to work from, because it gives tone reference and doesn't influence my choice of colours.

DW Your tracings are very detailed. Why?

PA Before I start to airbrush, I mask out every shape, every detail, and then spray in stages – I take the mask off in sections,

BARCLAYS BANK/THE ARTIST

BARCLAYS BANK/THE ARTIST

LEFT **The artist's finished trace of the artwork for the point-of-sale leaflet.**

BELOW **The art director's rough and final artwork of the 'shopping' poster. Paul Allen changed the size of the hands to improve the composition.**

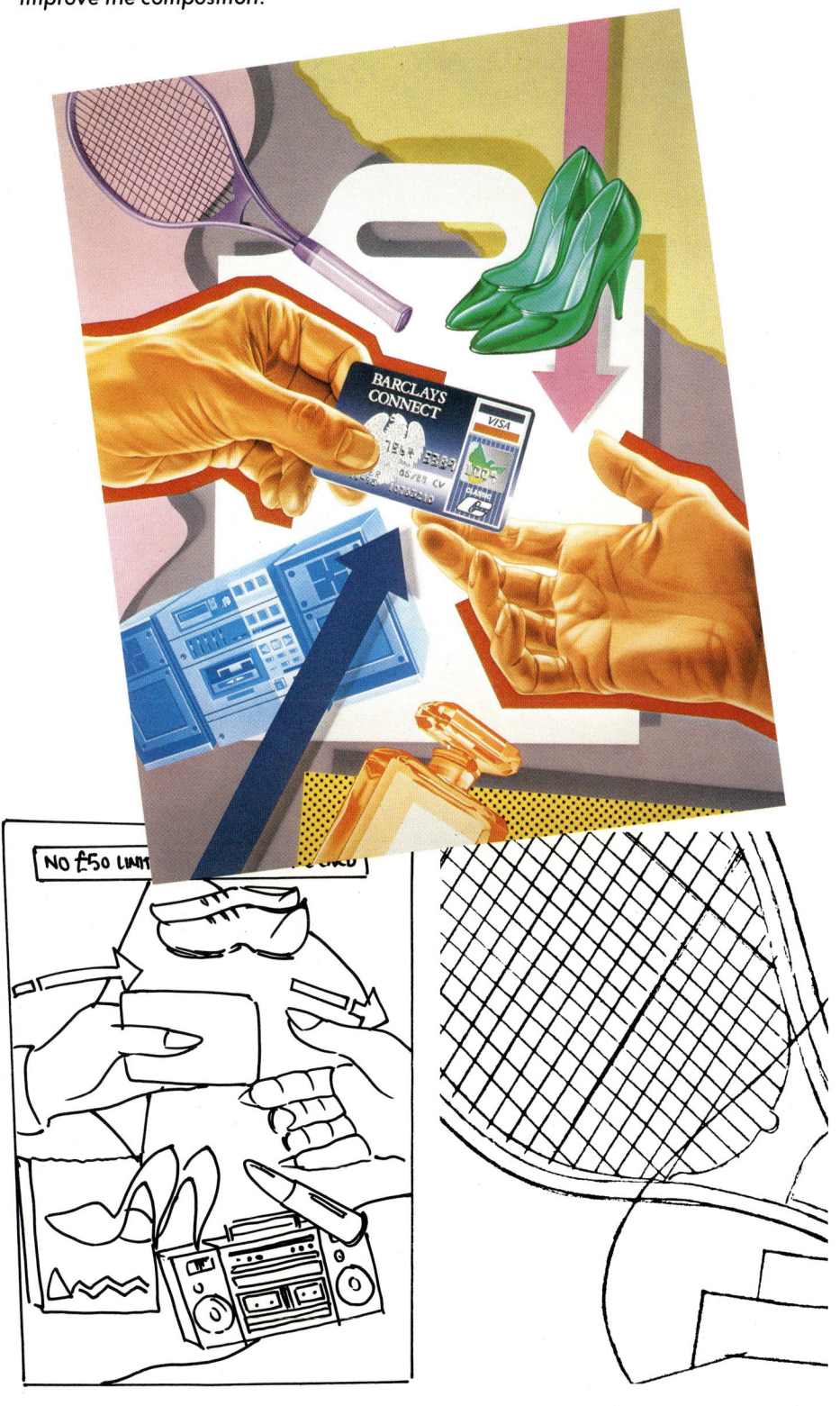

spray that section, take off the next piece, and so on. I spray each section lightly to give the shape and form of the object, and as I continue to spray and the colour is built up, the edges get softened.
DW Once you've constructed the drawing and you're ready to start painting, how do you work out the colour balance? Do you do the background first and then the main object?
PA I prefer to colour individual objects and then link the background to them. But I don't work colours out as such! I know what effect I want and I know my palette and how to use it.
DW With airbrushing it is possible to do the foreground first and then the background – in most mediums it's the other way round.
PA Yes. I had an overall colour scheme in mind, but the dominant image is the card with the hand. Throughout all the drawings the card is non-variable, so that's the starting point. The hands were important too; they needed strength and vibrancy as well as texture. Once that central image was done the atmosphere was set for the whole illustration.
DW You use very accurate reference prints for the hands, but do you ever find that the camera lies and the photographic image just doesn't look right?
PA Sometimes, but when I have to change the image it's usually more to do with what the client wants more than whether the pose is correct or not.
DW What materials do you use?
PA A combination of inks and acrylics. I never use gouache. I find them weak and powdery.
DW Do you favour ink or acrylic?
PA I used to do all my work in about six basic inks but they seem to have deteriorated over the last few years and got weaker. So I stopped using them on their own and included acrylics as well.
DW Do you intermix them – or put ink over the acrylic, or the acrylic over the ink?
PA I don't have a set method – sometimes I'll mix them but usually I'll use a specific paint for a specific colour, often straight from the tube. If that's not

15

BARCLAYS BANK/THE ARTIST

right I'll adjust it with inks – I tend to use whatever is necessary to arrive at my final colour.
DW Don't you ever find that there are problems in putting acrylics through the airbrush?
PA No, no problems at all, as long as you remember to clean it out!
DW What colours do you use for flesh tones?
PA I have a very non-textbook mix of colours. For flesh tones I usually mix red and black to give a dark brown – similar to Vandyke brown. I do all the dark tones in that, then, depending on the type of tones I need, I'll build up the rest of the colours. I often change quite a lot as I'm drawing – I might start with a mixture of orange and pink, then go to a brown and orange mix, just slowly building up the tone. One thing you have to watch with inks is that they have a strange ability to change colour when they're watered down – they don't just become a lighter version of the same colour, they tend to go more yellow.
DW How do you do the highlights?
PA I keep the highlights in mind when I'm airbrushing and then I'll use a typist's eraser.
DW Do you ever use a scalpel (utility knife) to 'knife' your highlights?
PA Sometimes I'll use a scalpel for really white highlights, because white paint often bleeds through if you're working over dyes. This can work to your advantage if you want a soft light, but is a nuisance if a really white light is needed. Using a scalpel is the easiest method then.
DW Do you paint by hand at all?
PA I might just use hand work to tidy up a little at the end of an illustration.
DW So your work is precise enough not to need coloured pencils or anything like that to touch up?
PA Yes, if I'm using an airbrush, I try to avoid using other methods like pencil. I like to keep the drawing pure airbrush as much as possible – even though I don't really see myself as an airbrush illustrator! In fact I try to avoid jobs that are obviously for the airbrush.

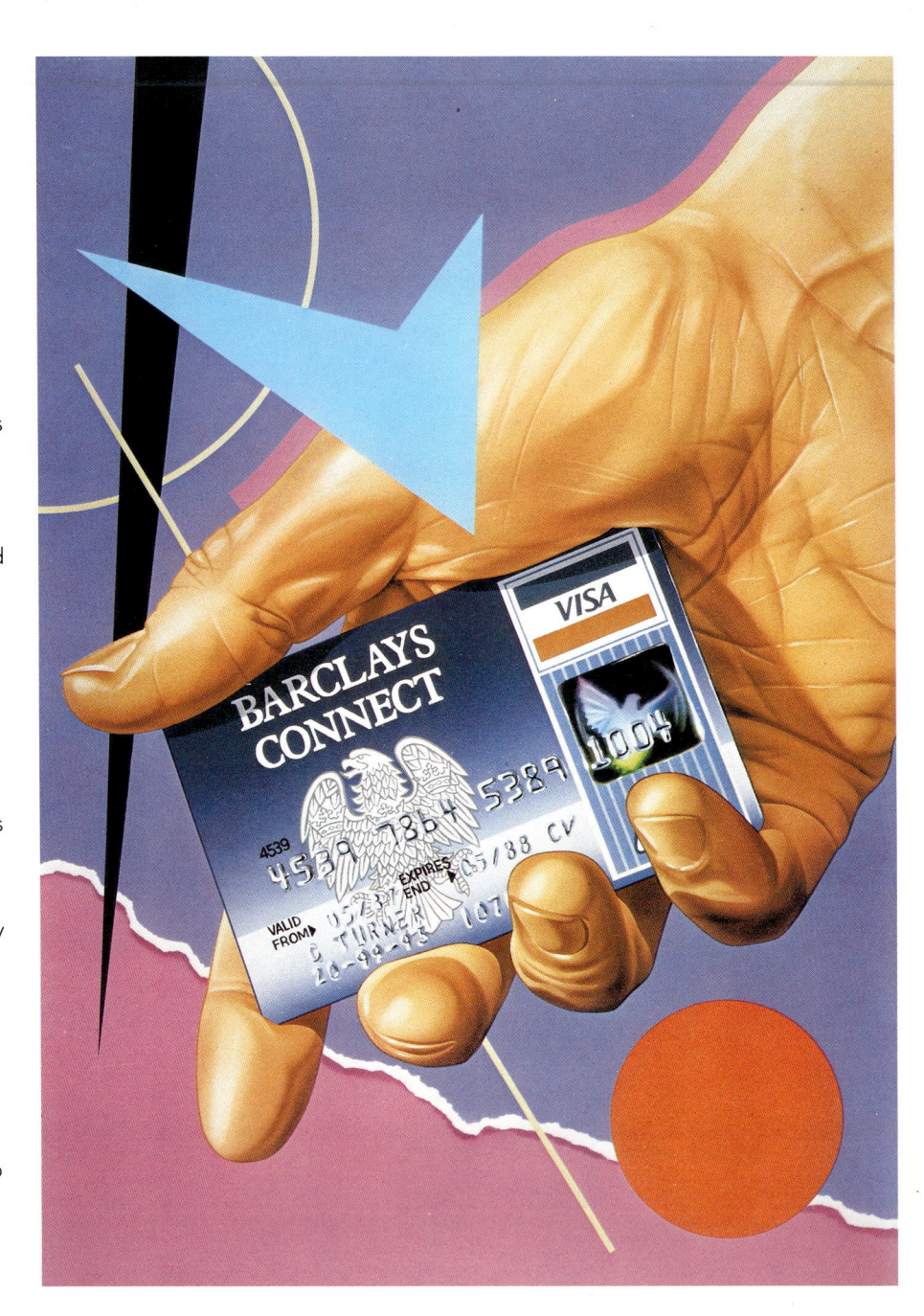

The finished artwork for the front cover of the point-of-sale leaflet and poster. Some late changes were made to this before printing: the hologram on the card was changed and the lines on the hand softened.

BARCLAYS BANK/THE ARTIST

RIGHT **Booking theatre seats over the telephone or in person: two uses of the product. The clever use of the theatrical masks immediately suggests entertainment.**

BELOW **The cashpoint poster. Here, the emphasis is on the convenience of modern technology.**

BELOW RIGHT **Another poster from the campaign with a bold illustration and strong copy line, stressing the advantages of the product.**

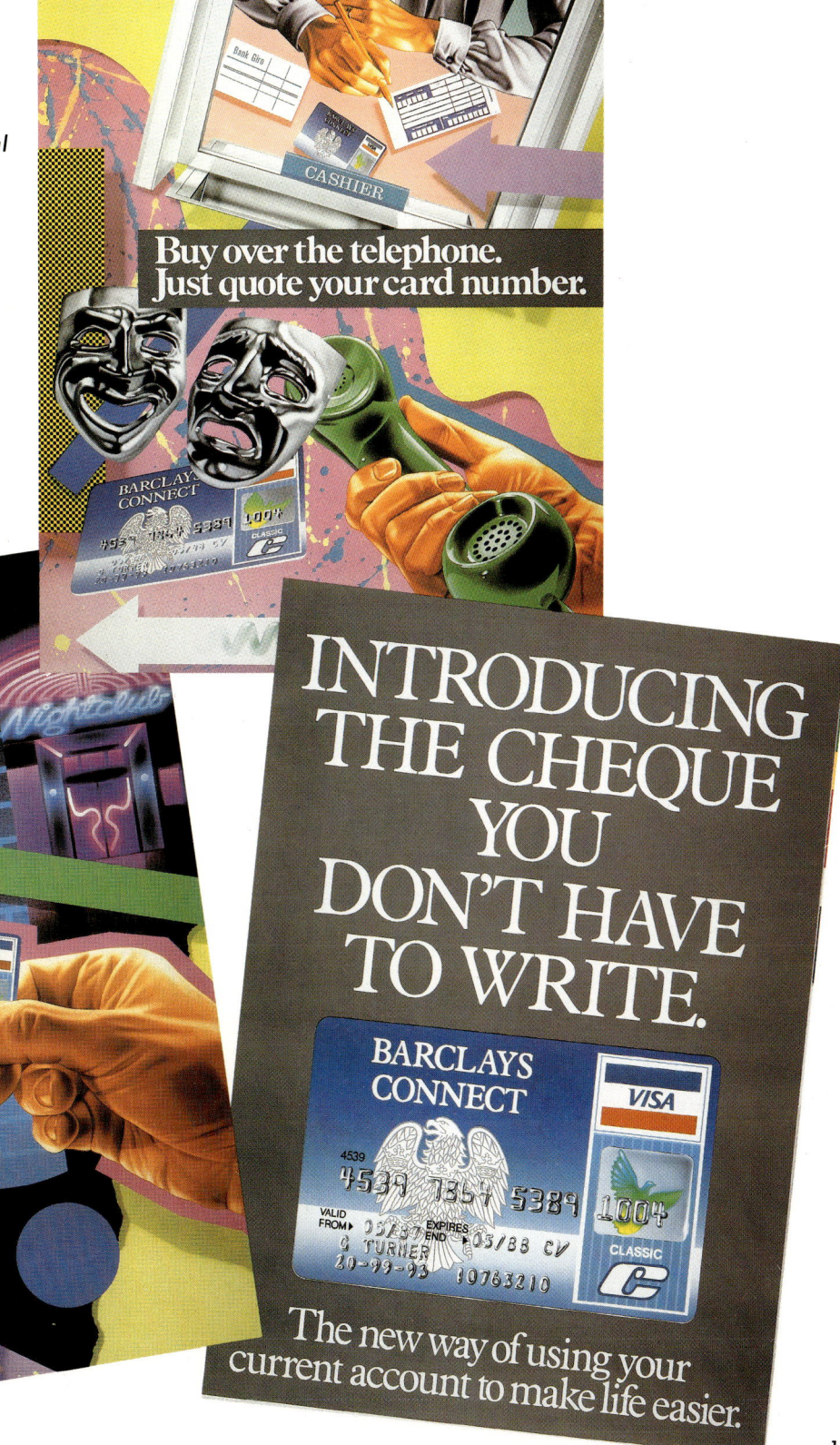

BARCLAYS BANK/AIRBRUSH

Paul Allen is a very competent draughtsman who can tackle any subject and achieve a superb finish in his work. The fearless way he uses strong inks straight from the bottle is a sign of an artist who understands his medium precisely.

Paul Allen works on a good-quality line board, which is normal practice for most airbrush illustrators, but his method of tracing down the image and masking out is unusual. He puts the adhesive masking film on the board first and then traces the image down. This method means there are no marks from the tracing-down paper on the board, which is an advantage as they can be difficult to remove.

This artist is well known for his illustrations of hands. In the demonstration he recreates the hand from the illustration used both as a poster (billboard) and as the front cover of the point-of-sale leaflet. The artist uses a combination of inks to achieve the flesh tones, and then overlays different transparent colours, slowly building up to the correct colour strength. He works straight from the bottles and sometimes actually mixes the colour in the airbrush.
The principle of using transparent inks is similar to the printing process: when one colour is laid over another it creates a third.
Most airbrush artists use a typist's eraser to bring out soft highlights. On a smooth surface board it is better to rub a highlight than to spray over existing colour. With white paint the base colour tends to show through and it is almost impossible to achieve a strong white. This is particularly so when inks or dyes are being used; it is easier to put white over acrylic paint, and in fact most acrylic painters work from dark to light (see Acrylic).

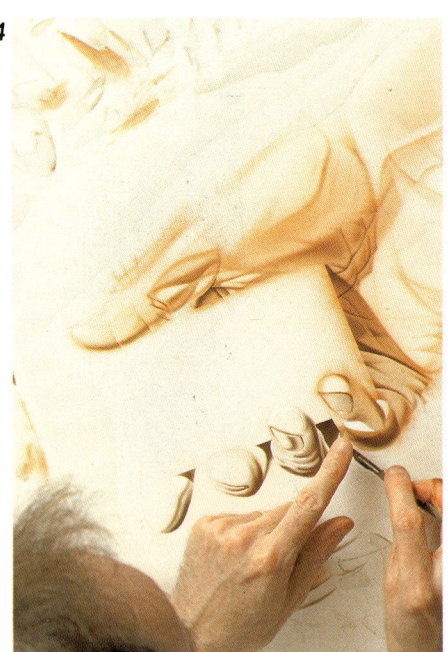

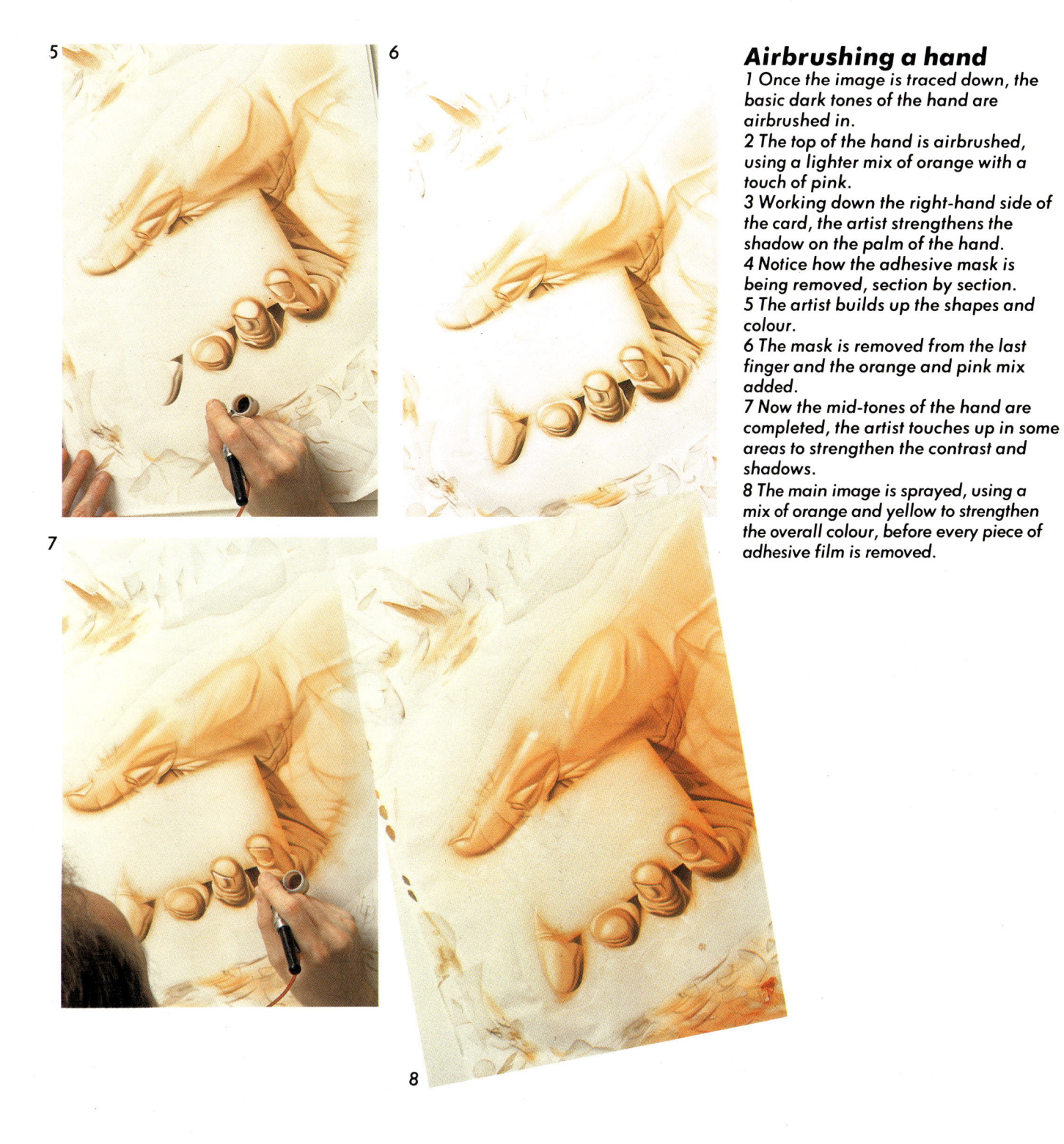

BARCLAYS BANK/THE TECHNIQUES

Airbrushing a hand

1 Once the image is traced down, the basic dark tones of the hand are airbrushed in.
2 The top of the hand is airbrushed, using a lighter mix of orange with a touch of pink.
3 Working down the right-hand side of the card, the artist strengthens the shadow on the palm of the hand.
4 Notice how the adhesive mask is being removed, section by section.
5 The artist builds up the shapes and colour.
6 The mask is removed from the last finger and the orange and pink mix added.
7 Now the mid-tones of the hand are completed, the artist touches up in some areas to strengthen the contrast and shadows.
8 The main image is sprayed, using a mix of orange and yellow to strengthen the overall colour, before every piece of adhesive film is removed.

BARCLAYS BANK/THE TECHNIQUES

The background

The backgrounds contain several different graphic symbols that can be created using a simple technique. But it takes an experienced artist to decide where and when, and how many of these symbols make up a successful composition.

1 The finished hand. A fresh sheet of adhesive film is laid ready for the next stage.
2 Using a piece of pink tracing-down paper, the background shapes are marked on the adhesive film. The hand, the arrowhead and the other shapes to be protected are carefully cut round and the area to be sprayed is revealed.
3 A sheet of cartridge (drawing) paper is torn for use as a mask. Then, with a little mounting spray, the smaller piece is tacked on to the board to make the ragged edge that runs at an angle across the base of the illustration. Then the blue part of the background is sprayed using acrylic paint, using the larger side of the torn paper to mask the blue.
4 The illustration is then turned round to spray the pink.
The section that is to be sprayed pink is cleaned with lighter fluid to remove all traces of mounting spray.
5 To spray the thin shadow that runs under the tear, two pieces of paper are used — they are moved slightly to give perspective. The artist uses a watered-down black with a touch of pink, which helps the colour blend slightly into the background.

All that remains to be done now is the other graphic shapes, using another adhesive mask, and the card. These will be drawn in the same way as any semi-technical drawing: the background sprayed first and then the lettering and details painted in by hand.

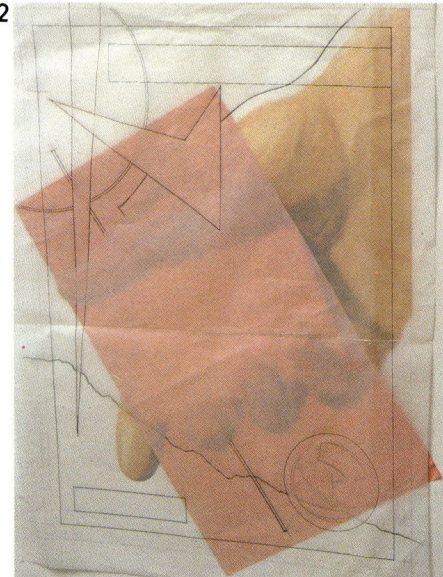

BARCLAYS BANK/THE TECHNIQUES

Graphic shapes

Much of Paul Allen's work uses graphic devices such as triangles, arrows, and panels of dots. Here he is creating a simple panel of yellow on a blue background, with a semi-soft shadow.

1 This time the image is traced on the board in the orthodox way, then adhesive film is laid over. The rectangle is masked out, and the outside of the blue background is also defined. A moveable mask is made of the rectangle using draw-film, ready for the semi-soft shadow. The artist is starting to spray the blue background, which he will build up to the desired strength.
2 The moveable mask is taped in position for the shadow. It is important not to stick the moveable mask to the drawing as the edge would become hard, not semi-soft.
3 The reverse of the original adhesive mask is replaced to cover the blue area in preparation for spraying the yellow.
4 All the masks are removed before the adhesive dot film is placed on the drawing and cut to shape.
5 The film is burnished down with a burnisher or the end of a paint brush.

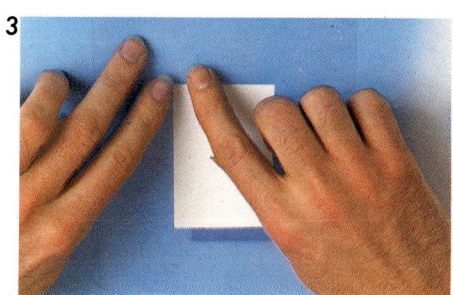

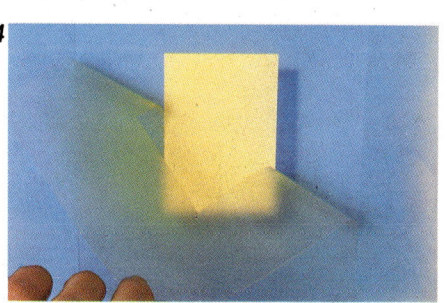

21

BORG-WARNER CHEMICALS/*THE CLIENT BRIEF*

THE CLIENT BORG WARNER CHEMICALS
THE BRIEF TO CREATE A TRADE CAMPAIGN TO SELL HIGH STANDARD PLASTIC ENGINEERING SERVICES WORLD-WIDE
THE AGENCY McCANNS INDUSTRIEEL
ART DIRECTOR DICK BERCKENKAMP
COPYWRITER HAN VAN WEL
ARTIST GEOFF NICHOLSON

This European trade campaign created by a Dutch agency is directed primarily at Britain, Germany and France, with simultaneous media coverage in Scandinavia and Italy. A campaign of this nature aimed at the trade rather than the general public requires the same amount of creative thinking behind it as a high-profile retail campaign. The product, ABS engineering plastics, is already the market leader and the campaign is designed to reinforce this position. ABS plastics are used in products such as the Swatch watches and car dashboards; the client also wanted to stress the customer-orientated engineering service offered. This campaign has set a trend, with the client's competitors following the style to sell their products. It also highlights the importance of being creative with trade campaigns and making attractive and informative ads.

A proof of the finished 'watches' ad. The overall effect of this painting is very strong with the hard shapes of the watches juxtaposed with a brilliantly illuminated street scene.

BORG-WARNER CHEMICALS/THE CLIENT BRIEF

housings for business machines, to dashboards
moulding for watch design be beyond us?

Borg-Warner Chemicals customers choose Cycolac® ABS for blow moulded housings – purely for the significant cost savings, lower production cycles and new design freedoms.

Car designers are employing more glass, by creating sharply raked windscreens, exposing dashboards to higher temperatures; dashboards moulded from high-heat resistant Cycolac® grades. And today, certain grades of this versatile engineering plastic are being applied to precision watch casings: revolutionizing the watch industry with colour and style.

Borg-Warner Chemicals' technical expertise and engineering thermoplastics have been changing design ideas, in everything from cars to computers. Can this be a sign of the times we live in?

BorgWarner Chemicals

We're everywhere, wherever you need us.

BORG-WARNER CHEMICALS/THE CLIENT BRIEF

Interview with Dick Berckenkamp

DICK BERCKENKAMP Before we started the campaign, the whole atmosphere surrounding plastics appeared to be foggy. We had to lift that atmosphere, reinforce the client as market leader and sell the product to an informed audience – designers, engineers and so on.
DICK WARD Do you use illustration often?
DB No, I normally use photography. But it would have been difficult, if not impossible, to get the effect I wanted with photography.
DW What alternative ideas did you have?
DB The first idea contained people wearing watches, but it was felt this was confusing because the product can be used for more than just watches. It would have seemed as if we were selling watches.
DW How did you arrive at the final image?
DB I wanted to find a surreal image because the product has multiple applications, and I felt the first ads were too specific and were too similar to each other.
DW How did you find the artist?
DB Through his agent.
DW You had no qualms about using an artist from another country?
DB No, it is very common in Holland for art directors to use overseas artists.
DW What was your timing on the whole job, from concept to finish?
DB About a year! The 'satellite dish' ad was the first one, then the 'car' and the 'dentist's chair'. After that we went for a more surreal approach as the first ads looked almost technical.
DW But aren't you selling to an informed audience?
DB Yes, but we wanted to be more adventurous – there is no reason, even if you're selling a technical product, not to produce an exciting picture.
DW Has the campaign been successful?
DB It appears so, from the feedback

BORG-WARNER CHEMICALS/THE ARTIST

OPPOSITE *The art director's alternatives for the watch ad.*

BELOW *The rough supplied to the illustrator allowed him considerable input.*

we've had from designers and engineers in the plastics trade.

Interview with Geoff Nicholson

DICK WARD What was your brief?
GEOFF NICHOLSON To draw a New York scene at night.
DW Did the agency supply the reference?
GN I was given a transparency for atmosphere, plus a watch and a catalogue, and a briefing on size.
DW Did you have a rough?
GN They sent a crude marker scribble.
DW On your original trace you've included cars and people.

GN Yes, but I took them out because the art director felt it would look more surreal without anything detracting from the watches.
DW Do you trace down on the board?
GN Yes, using red or grey tracing-down paper on standard line board.
DW As a general rule, how do you approach a drawing?
GN I normally do the blacks first and then work through to the darks. But with a drawing of this size, I'll do it in sections. My basic method is to draw the whole thing in black and tints of black. When that's done I use the inks to colour the whole drawing, and then finally I put in all the highlights with

either gouache, scalpel (utility knife) or erasers.
DW Do you mask out the outside edges of your drawing?
GN Yes, I like to keep it clean and see the final shape of it.
DW How long did you have for this particular drawing?
GN One day for the trace and about four or five for the drawing.
DW What materials do you use?
GN Waterproof inks and gouache.
DW Do you find gouache strong enough to use over the ink?
GN Yes. I use gouache to pick out highlights.
DW Doesn't the ink bleed through?

BORG-WARNER CHEMICALS/THE ARTIST

The artist's first working trace contains cars and people which were deleted in the final version.

GN No. As they're waterproof I don't find any problems. I also use them in reverse order – on this particular drawing, when I did the red lights of the cars in the street, I sprayed all the lights in with white gouache and then went over them with red ink – as the inks are transparent they don't affect the black, they just colour up the white.
DW What about highlights?
GN I use gouache over the inks for an airbrushed highlight and use the normal method of a scalpel and various different erasers for other highlights.
DW Do you use any handwork?
GN Yes, I use a brush and handwork to tidy up. On this drawing I've used brush ruling to finish off the windows on the building.
DW What do you use for reference shots?
GN Sometimes I'll use a polaroid, but they tend to be too small so I take 35mm shots. It doesn't hold me up since it's possible to get them processed very quickly these days.
DW Do you use colour, or black and white film?
GN Colour.
DW Do you use a copyscanner (Camera Lucida).
GN Not very often. I use a photocopying machine that can enlarge – so I copy my reference shots or my trace up to the size I want.
DW The photocopy you've used for this job has been cut up quite a lot. Why is that?
GN Sometimes I'll cut a shape out of it to make a soft edge. It saves tracing down another image on a piece of paper or film and obviously it's exactly the right shape.
DW What else do you use for masking?
GN Adhesive film is my main mask and virtually anything else that comes to hand that's suitable! I'll use french curves or templates for softer edges.

BORG-WARNER CHEMICALS/THE TECHNIQUES

The artwork at the final stage before the rest of the buildings are completed.

Geoff Nicholson's basic technique breaks the whole process of airbrush drawing down to its simplest form. All the blacks on the drawing are normally put in first. Here, as the drawing is large, Geoff Nicholson has divided it into sections. This requires a lot of skill since the artist must maintain the colour balance as the drawing progresses. The technique relies on the transparency of the waterproof inks as Geoff Nicholson works from black through to dark and finally 'colours up' the drawing in a method similar to tinting a photograph. With a drawing of this nature, it is important to have an accurate trace, because the vanishing points and the perspective would look totally wrong if they were just a fraction out. When drawing buildings, or any similar objects involving squares, rectangles or rigid geometric shapes with exact dimensions, the size is taken from the leading edge and the vanishing point will do the rest. In this case, Geoff Nicholson has worked out the dimensions of the windows on the foremost edges of the buildings and his vanishing point is somewhere left of centre of the distant cluster of buildings. The sky background is put in first, to set the tone values of the whole drawing.

THE BUILDINGS

Once the buildings are drawn in, the artist painstakingly masks out every window with adhesive film and then sprays them one by one, starting with the darkest, moving on to the next lightest, and so on. By the time the lightest windows are reached, all the window masks have been removed; the lightest window receives just a whiff of ink to give a little colour. The verticals and some of the horizontals are put in by hand using brush ruling.

THE ROAD

Here the artist has masked out the road to the hardest edge, in this case the pavement (sidewalk). A solid black is sprayed on and then the highlights of the cars are sprayed using gouache. Sometimes the airbrush is run along a ruler to maintain a straight line, the same method as brush ruling. The red is added using ink which, being transparent, merely tints the white and does not affect the black. The soft edge on the pavement is then sprayed without remasking – the airbrush is held close to the board to control the spread of colour. The brightly lit windows are the white support with a very light touch of ink to give a little colour and form inside. The light thrown on to the pavement from the windows is sprayed on using a moveable straight edge made from cartridge paper. The street lights are added with freehand airbrush using white gouache.

THE WATCHES

Geoff Nicholson draws in the watches using the basic technique; the solid black is put in first, then the masks are removed as the other colours are added. The gold motifs on the base of the right-hand watch face are sprayed in ink over the black, without the black being masked out – likewise the pink face. The other details, such as the hands and the shadows, are added either by hand or by using the photocopy as a mask – the edge on the body of the watch is masked in this way. The straps are drawn in using an adhesive mask for the hard edges. A combination of french curves and shapes cut from the photocopy are used for the darker shapes on the face. The reflections on the glass face are added last of all using a scalpel (utility knife) and a typist's eraser to scratch away highlights.

BORG-WARNER CHEMICALS/ACRYLIC

The watch

Geoff Nicholson uses a combination of methods to create the watch face. The master photocopy is used as a mask; this saves time, as the artist doesn't have to trace the required shape down on another piece of paper, and is accurate because the original image is being used.

The background

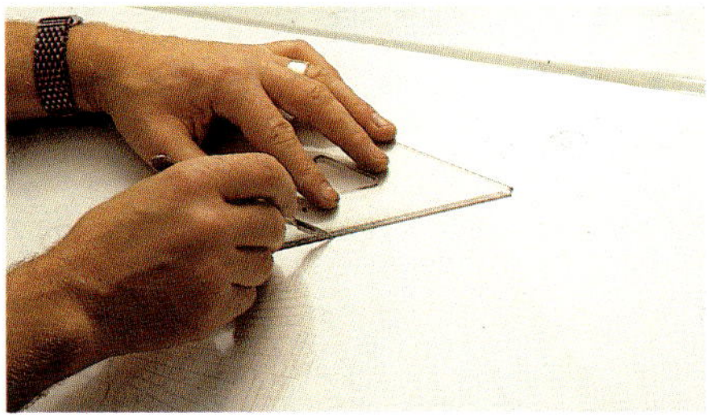

1
The first adhesive mask is cut so that the background can be sprayed.

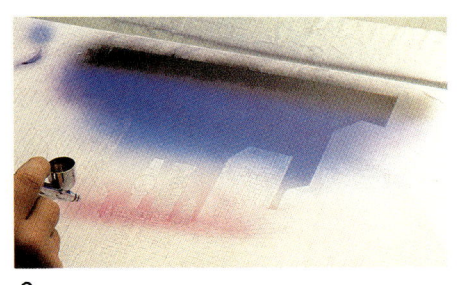

1
The artist prepares the mask for the solid blacks on the watch face.

4
The yellow is sprayed. As Geoff Nicholson uses transparent colour, the black is not affected by the yellow and need not be masked.

2
The artist sprays the dark blue first. He uses a hairdryer to ensure that no colour seeps under the mask.

2
He starts to spray the black, using a hairdryer to stop the colour bleeding under the mask.

5
The artist uses the photocopy as a mask to spray the edge of the watch. This achieves a semi-soft edge and ensures accuracy.

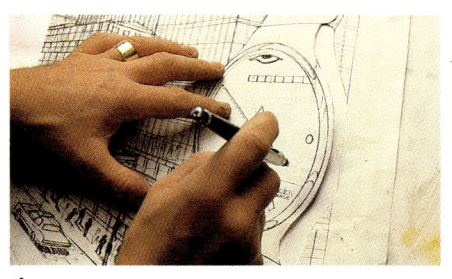

3
He has built up the blue and is adding black at the top and pink at the bottom.

3
Now the mask covering the front of the strap is removed and the strap is sprayed.

6
The edge is sprayed in a slightly darker colour to that at the front.

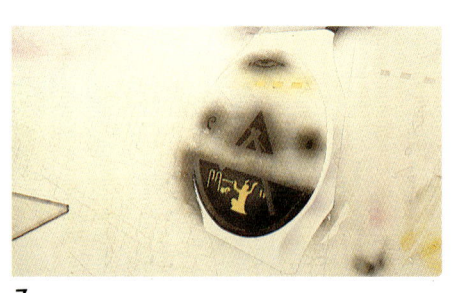

7
The mask is replaced over the watch strap and the front face of the watch rim is exposed.

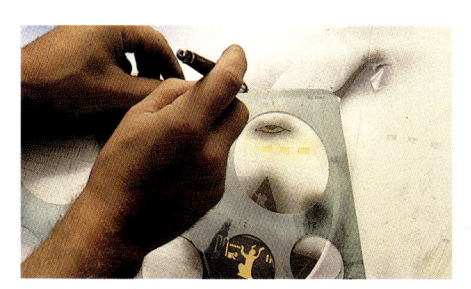

BORG-WARNER CHEMICALS/THE TECHNIQUES

8
Using a template as a mask, the artist begins to spray the watch rim. The next stage is to finish the watch face and the rest of the strap.

9
The mask is replaced over the watch casing.

10
The mask is removed from the rim of the glass.

11
The darker pinks are put in first, and the second hand is sprayed in a dark pink.

12
Geoff Nicholson moves on to the lower strap which is sprayed in the same way as the top strap.

13
A new adhesive mask is laid. Geoff Nicholson uses a set square to smooth down the adhesive film.

14
The watch face is exposed, with the small coloured rectangles and the eye motif masked out.

15
The photocopy is laid over the face to act as a semi-soft mask as the drop shadows on the hands are sprayed on.

16
The main watch face is coloured a soft pink, and the soft shadow around the far edge of the glass is sprayed in using a perspex template.

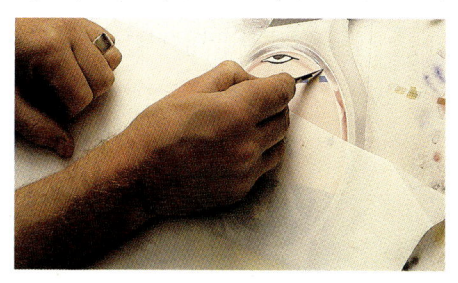

17
The mask is removed and a scalpel is used to create some strong highlights on the edge of the glass face.

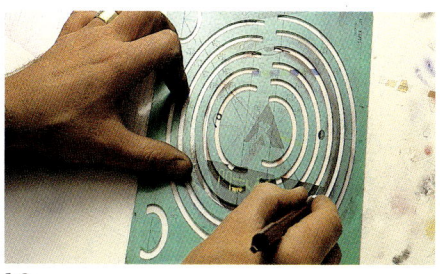

18
A perspex template and a technical pen are used to strengthen the edge of the glass face.

19
The finished watchface. The winding nob on the right has been added by hand.

BORG-WARNER CHEMICALS/ACRYLIC

The road

The buildings

1
Geoff Nicholson replaces the sky mask and begins to cut the mask for the front of the building. He has masked out the darkest parts of the building and begins to spray them first.

2
He removes some of the masks over the windows to spray the next stage. Now he begins to do the same on the front of the building, exposing the windows that are to be the darkest.

3
He sprays the windows, keeping unwanted colour off adjacent windows by the use of a hand-held paper mask.

4
The tone is graduated on each window by carefully confining the colour to one part of each segment.

5
The masks are removed for the next stage.

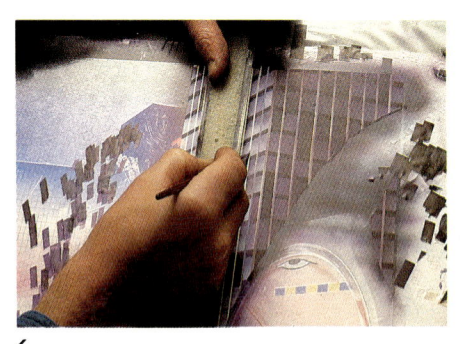

6
The front of the building is sprayed. The vertical lines at the front are exposed and painted in by hand using a brush-ruling technique.

The road area is masked out to the edge of the pavement and then sprayed in a solid black. The highlights are sprayed over using white gouache, then the colour is added with ink.

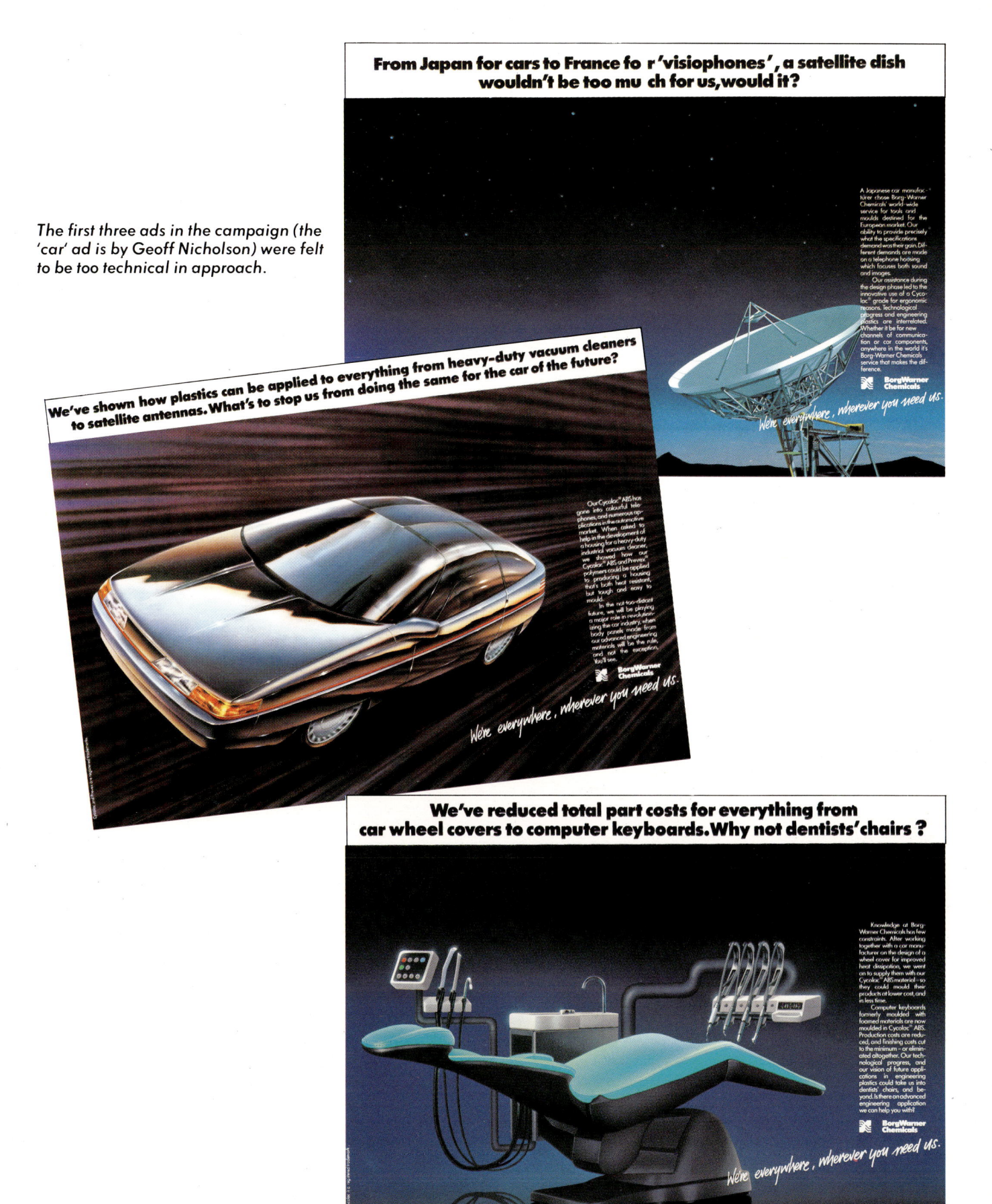

BORG-WARNER CHEMICALS/THE TECHNIQUES

The first three ads in the campaign (the 'car' ad is by Geoff Nicholson) were felt to be too technical in approach.

From Japan for cars to France for 'visiophones', a satellite dish wouldn't be too much for us, would it?

We've shown how plastics can be applied to everything from heavy-duty vacuum cleaners to satellite antennas. What's to stop us from doing the same for the car of the future?

We've reduced total part costs for everything from car wheel covers to computer keyboards. Why not dentists' chairs?

C. NEWTON
GIFTS
TAILOR
FREE
HOUSE
DAWES FISHING TACKLE
THE ROXBURGH ARMS
HALIFAX BUILDING SOCIETY

ACRYLIC

Acrylic paints for artists' use have only been available since the early 1960s. Before that artists made their own by mixing domestic acrylic emulsion base with pigments – they recognized the advantages of a fast-drying water-based paint that was resistant to water and could be applied to almost any surface. Although the same pigments are used in acrylic as in oil paints, true alizarin crimson, Prussian blue and viridian green cannot be produced as the acrylic base is too alkaline to mix with these pigments. All acrylic paints have a degree of opacity; they are widely used in commercial work. It is possible to use them to achieve a convincing imitation of an oil painting, and their quick-drying qualities make them very practical for the modern illustrator. They are also versatile enough to be used through the airbrush.

Acrylic painting by Anne Sharp for the Halifax Building Society.

BELL'S WHISKY/THE CLIENT BRIEF

THE CLIENT BELL'S WHISKY
THE BRIEF TO STRENGTHEN THE IMAGE OF BELL'S AS A QUALITY BRAND OF WHISKY, AND TO MAINTAIN ITS POSITION AS MARKET LEADER
THE AGENCY LOWE HOWARD SPINK
ART DIRECTOR DAVE CHRISTENSEN
ARTIST TOM ADAMS

A campaign that is all about quality needs a very subtle approach. With this kind of advertising, the idea is to reinforce the position of the brand as market leader. The effect on the consumer is almost subliminal and only if Bell's stopped advertising altogether could the effect on sales – and, thus, the effectiveness of the campaign – be measured. The same is true of leading brands in all products.

People often claim that they're not affected by advertising, but if the total coverage were reduced, the brand would slowly drop from the consumer's awareness. It is no coincidence that brand leaders remain brand leaders, and they do it not only by maintaining the quality of the product but by constantly battling to keep their name in the customer's mind. In the US, for example, it is common for a customer to ask for a brand name rather than just a scotch, a situation that European manufacturers are trying to encourage. But the problem is that although everyone has heard of Bell's they have also heard of at least a dozen other brands.

The task of the agency is to strengthen the idea of Bell's as a quality product while keeping the client's brand in the consumer's mind at all times. To this end, art director Dave Christensen chose a highly skilled artist to reflect the quality of the product.

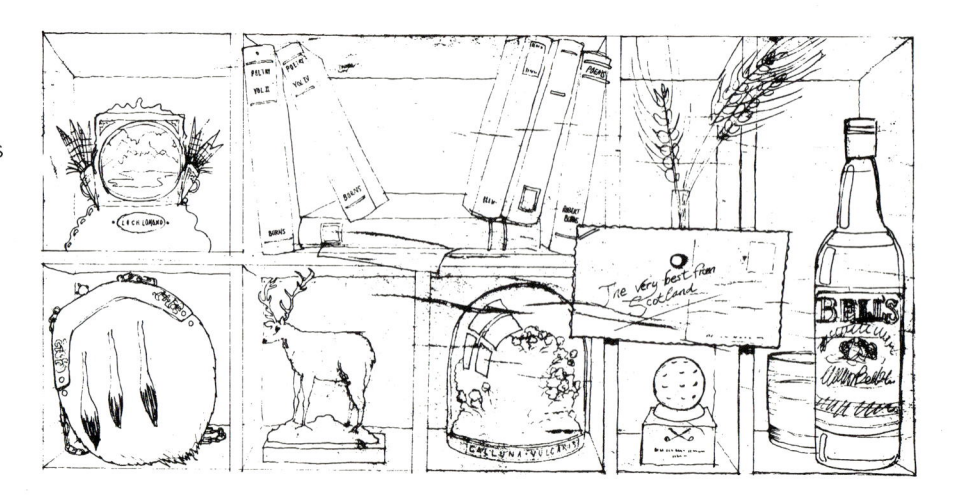

BELL'S WHISKY/THE CLIENT BRIEF

TOP *The finished 72-sheet poster (billboard).*

BELOW LEFT *The first rough produced by the agency.*

BELOW RIGHT *A more finished pencil rough by the illustrator Graham Berry.*

Interview with Dave Christensen

DICK WARD What was the exact brief from your client?
DAVE CHRISTENSEN To come up with a poster and an international ad to emphasize the traditions and quality of Scotch whisky, and in particular of Bell's and, at the same time, make it more appealing to younger people. Bell's is such a well-known brand that it had ceased to be special anymore. We had to upgrade its image. The *trompe l'oeil* style has the visual impact that appeals to young people. You don't have to go out and shout 'Hey, young people, this is for you!'

35

BELL'S WHISKY/THE ARTIST

DW And it was designed with different formats in mind?
DC Yes, we designed it for a 72-sheet and 48-sheet poster (billboard) as well as a double-page spread. It's designed to crop for each use along the line of the boxes.
DW There's no copy on this ad?
DC A little, but only on details like the postcard.
DW When were you briefed on it?
DC The brief was issued on the 20th October and I produced the first visual about the middle of November.
DW What did you give Tom to work from?
DC I did a scribble. That can be sufficient to show clients once you have established a rapport with them, but Bell's is a fairly recent client of ours, so I had a more finished rough done by Graham Berry.
DW Is he an artist who just does roughs?
DC No, he's a finished illustrator. I just liked his pencil drawings.
DW What did Tom come up with first of all?
DC He produced a great pencil drawing at the stage when we were working out exactly what sort of things we were going to include in the ads. The client took the objects in Tom's first drawing and made them into flashcards – a picture of the Monarch of the Glen, for example, or a picture of a piece of tartan – which they showed to selected groups of people. The test groups were asked: 'which 10 of these objects say Scotland to you?' Surprisingly enough, most of the people came up with more or less the same set of objects. That's how we arrived at the set of objects that were painted.
DW What made you choose illustration for this job?
DC It was obviously right for the kind of campaign. The whole thing would have been rather dead if it had been done photographically, and I think that doing it in a *trompe l'oeil* style gives it a slightly mysterious and deceptive feel, so the viewer is not quite sure what it means but is curious to find out. The puzzling element seems to appeal to younger people. A straight photograph wouldn't have had that attraction.

DW Do you think you have more control using illustration?
DC No, you probably have less, although I think in this case that's a good thing. It allows the illustrator quite a bit of input.
DW How did you hear of Tom Adams?
DC It was quite strange. There was a young man at Bell's who'd seen the visuals and heard we were looking far and wide for an illustrator. He mentioned his uncle and asked if we would like to look at his work, so we agreed. In all honesty, we weren't too hopeful, but he turned out to be exactly right.
DW That's an unusual way to find an artist and it's an unusual style for advertising.
DC Yes, but it worked extremely well and we hope to push it further as the campaign continues, so we establish a look. We could go on to other areas, such as notice boards, with bits and pieces slotted in behind tapes or pinned on.
DW How long is this campaign projected to last?
DC It could go on for over five years, with probably just two or three posters per year. It's not the kind of campaign where you have to produce an ad every week or month. It is a very visual approach that creates a lot of interest as there's so much to look at. After a while, the public makes the connection between the image or series of images and the product. And we always include a visual reference to our client – there will be a little bell in each one – and in this case, harebells, which are Scottish bluebells. So people start looking for any references to bells.

Interview with Tom Adams

DICK WARD How long were you given after the first brief?
TOM ADAMS We met at the end of the year and I was supposed to get started in January, but there were hold-ups, so it was mid-February before I actually started collecting all the objects I needed. I went to the Museum of Antiquities in Edinburgh to get a dirk and a sporran. Sporrans are about 40 cm (16 in) long, not the correct proportion to fit into the box. So I had to adapt a Gordon Highlander's sporran, and substitute a badge that has a connection with Bell's. Then I had to find the soldier, the glass – and the barley, which was a very difficult problem, as it was the middle of winter! Eventually we managed to track some down at a research station in Norfolk. All this ate into the painting time, of course.
DW How much time did you have?
TA I was supposed to deliver in mid-March, but I didn't start painting until the last week in February. I delivered on the 23rd March. About one week late.
DW Was the agency put out by that?
TA No, not really. They did realize how much preparatory work had to be done.
DW Once you'd assembled all the reference material, did you then make all the boxes, or was it the other way round?
TA A bit of both, as some of the objects were the correct size and others weren't. The books, for example, were much too big, so I had to make a box around them. All the boxes are of a different depth to accommodate everything correctly.
DW Did you employ a joiner or a carpenter to make the boxes?
TA No. I was going to, but the budget was too tight, so I made them. In fact it was easier that way, apart from the time factor, because with all the different sizes it would have been very complicated if I'd had to brief somebody.
DW The next stage, I presume, was to photograph it?
TA Yes. I'd produce an enormous number of photographs because I needed to see exactly where the shadows fell. On the dirk shot I photographed a mock-up, because I didn't have the actual object at that stage. Most of the items were photographed at separate times as I didn't have everything at once, but the lighting was kept the same. I always paint from the actual objects though. The photographs are just used as reference, particularly for the light.
DW What was your main style reference?
TA A painting by an artist called Alexander (Isadore) Leroy de Barde (1777-

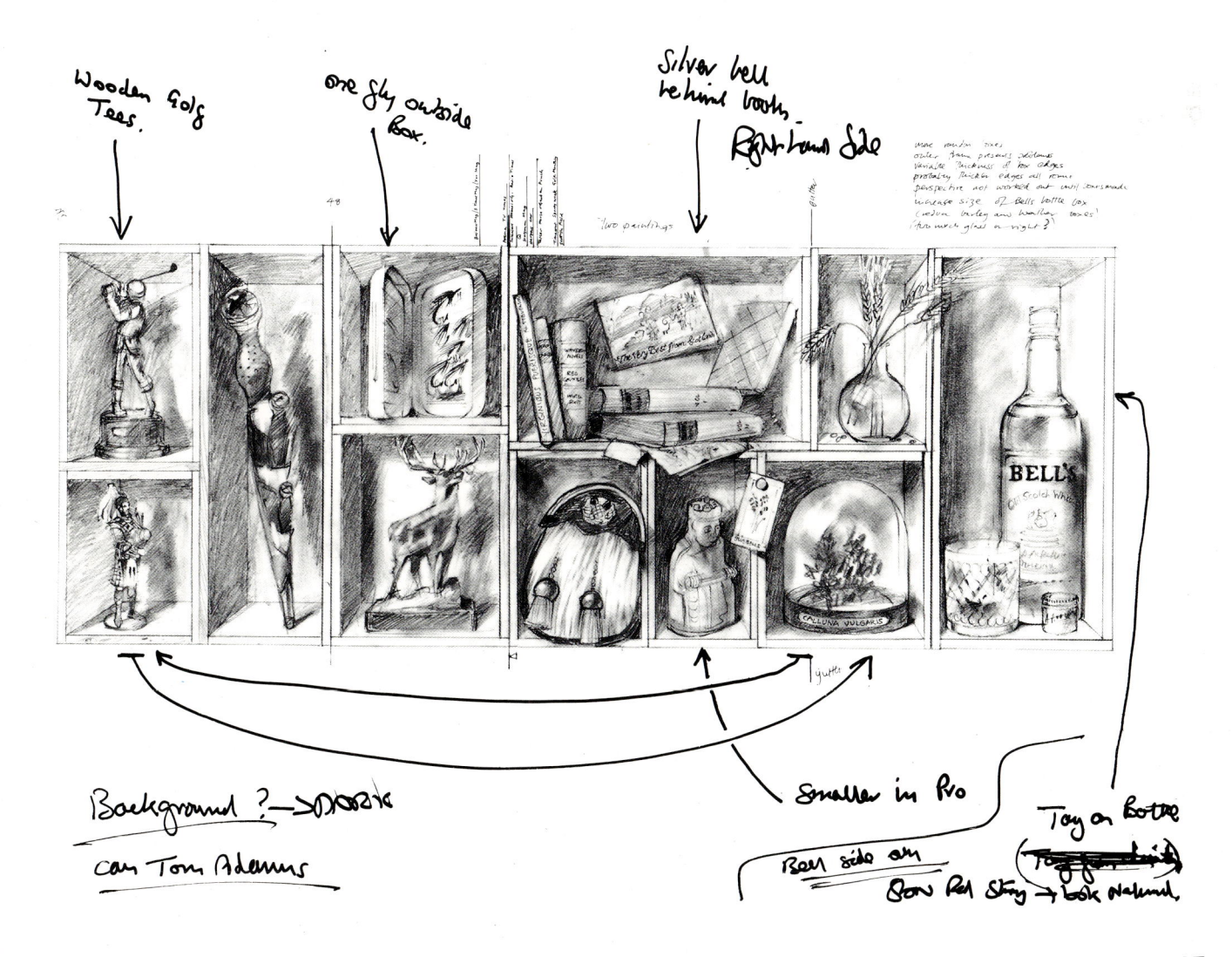

BELL'S WHISKY/THE ARTIST

LEFT Tom Adams built wooden boxes to accommodate the objects so that he had an accurate model to paint from.

BELOW The artist's working drawing with the art director's comments.

BELL'S WHISKY/THE FINISHED ARTWORK

1828), which I saw in a book called Trompe l'Oeil Painting: The Illusions of Reality by Miriam Milman.
DW How long do you think you spent on the actual painting?
TA I only had about three weeks left for it, which wasn't a great deal of time. I ended up working about 16 hours a day, so I was cramming two days' work into one. I usually worked at night because of the interruptions during the day.
DW Art directors tend to underestimate the actual logistics involved in getting all the bits and pieces together.
TA That's right. When there's a lot of research as well, it can take an awfully long time.
DW Do you find that when you're working at that kind of pace you sometimes just have to take a break and walk away from it, even if only for a short while?
TA Yes. Sometimes you get so stiff you just have to stop for a time.
DW Do you paint in sections or work on the whole picture?

TA I tend to work on it bit by bit, after laying the whole thing out. But I always do a really finished pencil drawing first. It might be a slow way round, and others may be able to work without it, but I've always found that its best to solve any problems that could crop up at the earliest stage possible.
DW Do you trace it down in the normal way using a copy scanner (Camera Lucida)?
TA No. I use the epidioscope (opaque projector), which projects the image directly on to the board – it saves time because there are no intervening stages as there are with a copy scanner. The only problem, of course, is you need to find a pretty dark corner for it, but as I was working at night on this it was ideal.
DW Did you paint it on canvas?
TA No. It's on good-quality drawing paper, a kind of cartridge paper, mounted on plywood.
DW How do you prepare the painting first of all?
TA I drew straight on to the paper and

fixed it, then did some of the early washes. After that, I put a coat of varnish over it, so I was really working on a varnished paper surface.
DW What did you stick the paper on the board with?
TA Just with paper paste, the kind used for wallpaper; it's the traditional type that doesn't stain and has a fungicide in it. I

BELL'S WHISKY/THE FINISHED ARTWORK

FAR LEFT One of the photographs taken by Tom Adams to show him where the shadows fell.

TOP CENTRE The model is in front of the artist's desk so that he can refer to it constantly.

BELOW CENTRE Tom Adams drawing.

LEFT The first section of the painting taking shape. The early washes have been laid and will be slowly built up to create rich, deep colours.

BELOW The completed first section.

39

BELL'S WHISKY/*THE FINAL IMAGE*

The flexibility of the design confirmed. A finished image on site, comprising the full first section with part of the second.

BELL'S WHISKY/THE TECHNIQUES

think it's still made from refined flour.
DW Do you put a light wash on first or do you work from dark to light?
TA I usually put the darks on first and work back to the light, referring to my drawing and the actual objects all the time.
DW I've noticed that your darks are particularly rich. How do you achieve this?
TA I use a retouching varnish. I put a thin coat over the darks at regular intervals throughout the painting. It gives a real richness and depth.
DW Then the last thing you put on are the white highlights?
TA Yes. I slowly build up the colours, lighter and lighter, and the final touches are the highlights. At various stages I use the retouching varnish very sparingly to add richness.
DW The lettering looks extremely professional.
TA Well, I'm not a lettering artist and it does take me a long time. If you look at it closely you'll see it's a bit wobbly! But it's meant to look the way an 18th-century *trompe l'oeil* artist would do it, so it can't be too perfect. The whole point of the campaign is to make it look like a genuine old master canvas. It would be wrong if it ended up looking like a photograph. I did have some problems with the lettering on the postcard as it didn't reproduce very well, so I had to paint it out with poster paints and it was dropped in mechanically.
DW Did you use an airbrush at all, in particular on the dark side of the bottle?
TA No. I tried an airbrush years ago but I never really got on with it, so I do it by hand.

This is a beautifully executed painting done by an artist with traditional skills that, sadly, are becoming rarer as years go by. From Tom Adams's viewpoint, this is a rewarding job, with plenty of exposure. If the amount of time the artist spent on the job were analyzed, it wouldn't necessarily be well paid, but, even for commercial illustrators, satisfaction with the job can be the most important motivation.

Tom Adams works on a good-quality cartridge (drawing) paper mounted on plywood, and battened at the back for extra strength. The surface is built up, first, by laying a coat of varnish and, during the painting, by constantly using retouching varnish which enriches the colours and gives the finished painting the depth of tone of a genuine old master.

The actual painting is quite small, bearing in mind the size of the finished ads, but the quality of the work is such that is can stand being greatly enlarged.

Tom Adams uses normal acrylics, but the retouching varnish gives a look of oil paint. Using actual oil paints in commercial work is hardly feasible because of the drying time.

The amount of commitment and the time spent is obvious in the finished painting — each object, and the pattern of the light and shade, has been carefully studied.

Although there is an enormous build up of colour on the original, there are no lumps or bumps on the surface of the painting as the paint is applied as a series of washes.

BELL'S WHISKY/ACRYLIC

WOOD GRAIN

Techniques for painting wood grain are similar to those used in Victorian times for decorating doors and panels with the then fashionable imitation graining; colours are kept necessarily simple, and the best results are obtained by observing and copying a particular piece of wood.

Colours obviously depend on the type of wood being painted. Here the palette consists mainly of pale yellows and light brownish reds, but different woods call for different mixtures. Mahogany, for example, contains a predominance of warm pinks and rich purple tones.

Successful wood graining depends on a simple procedure. The main colour is usually laid first, ready to receive light and dark graining patterns. For the purpose of this demonstration, the artist chose two pieces of wood – one with a light yellow base, the other a pale brownish red – similar to the shelf uprights in the Tom Adams painting. The graining is added when these initial colours are dry. Confidence is essential here. Once a line has been started, it is difficult to stop or break off half way without losing the organic flowing quality of the line.

The graining is painted in fairly thin colour with a fine sable brush. By altering the pressure on the loaded brush, the artist is able to vary the thickness of the line in order to reproduce the irregular and undulating patterns of natural wood. Because acrylic paints dry quickly and are insoluble once dry, one colour can be laid over another without fear of the top colour disturbing or running and bleeding into any of the colours underneath. This enables the artist to paint the wood grain as a series of crisp shapes over flat colour.

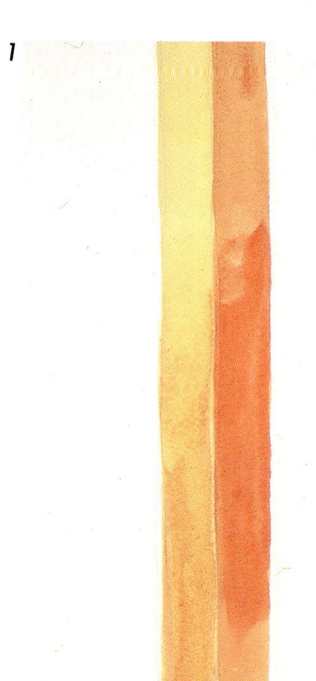

BELL'S WHISKY/THE TECHNIQUES

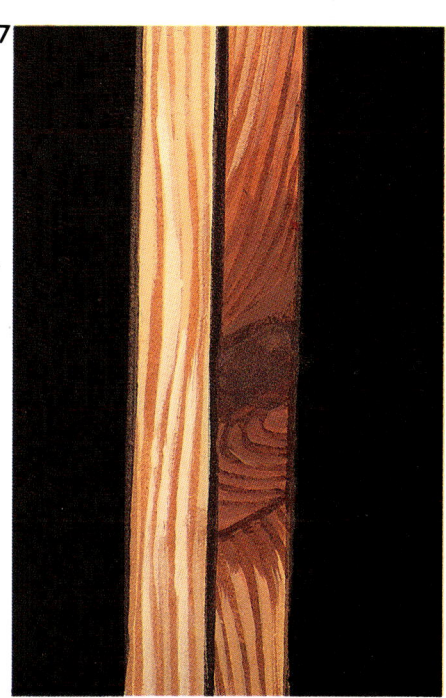

Wood grain

1 The base colours of the two wooden uprights are laid in washes of pale yellow and reddish brown respectively. A patch of darker colour is painted on the right-hand wood, anticipating the position of a knot.
2 Thin layers of flat black are built up to represent the shadowy recesses of the wooden boxes — the colour is taken up to, and slightly over, the edges of the wood in order to obtain a clean, crisp line.
3 A fine sable brush is used to paint the ruled line between the two wooden uprights. Notice how the artist holds the edge of the ruler slightly above the paper to prevent smudging.
4 The procedure so far is simple — just three blocks of almost flat colour divided by a ruled line. Yet already this picture has something of the feel of the finished painting, requiring merely the painted grain to complete the image.
5 Uneven, flowing lines are painted along the right-hand strip. The first series is in a slightly deeper version of the initial wash colour. The artist then lays paler lines in opaque light yellow, running these between the darker grains. Notice how the imposition of the light lines is inexact, and narrow strips of the basic wash are allowed to show through.
6 The grain of the second strip of wood is painted in exactly the same way, except that here the lines follow the shape of the knot. Once the paint is dry, the artist gives the painting a coat of retouching varnish to brighten up the colours.
7 The finished picture. The artist has taken care not to overwork the image — the effectiveness of this particular technique depends upon its simplicity.

BELL'S WHISKY/ACRYLIC

Reflections on glass

Acrylic paints are opaque enough to cover any underlying colour – even when painting white over black, one coat of fairly thick acrylic is sufficient to completely obliterate the dark tone underneath. This 'hiding' capacity makes acrylics the ideal medium for working from dark to light, as Tom Adams did in the Bell's painting.

Because he did not have to work out the colours of the painting in advance – a necessary stage when using transparent materials, such as inks or watercolours, since you have to work from light to dark – he was free to concentrate on the image itself, painting carefully and painstakingly from the actual subject instead of wrestling with the limitations of the medium.

Reflections lend themselves to the 'light over dark' approach, especially reflections on dark glass, or glass which is placed against a dark background, as is the case with the Bell's whisky bottle. The dark tones were established first, in broad, flat brushstrokes. Medium and lighter tones were then applied to build up the form of the bottle with planes of light and shade.

The final, almost white, highlights are important in bringing the image alive. Until that point, the bottle looks flat and matt. Without these very bright reflections, there is no indication that we are looking at a *glass* object – it is only the familiar shape of the bottle which gives it away. Although essential when rendering glass or another highly glossy surface, highlights must not be overdone. Their effectiveness depends on absolute accuracy – and their position should emphasize the form of the object, not contradict it.

Tom Adams uses retouching varnish, a resin-based medium which enlivens the characteristically dull, matt finish of acrylic paint. This varnish is not compatible with the paints, and so cannot be mixed with the actual colours. Instead, it is applied in a thin coat over the area being worked once the paint is completely dry. The varnish itself must be allowed to dry thoroughly before further painting can take place. Usually, no more than one or two layers are used in any one area of the painting. The result is a slightly glossy finish, not unlike the surface of an oil painting.

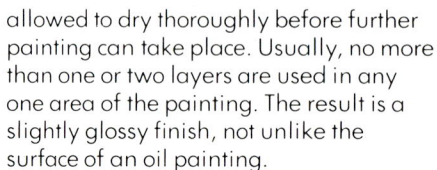

BELL'S WHISKY/THE TECHNIQUES

Reflections

1 The artist paints in the background first, to establish the colours which will be seen through the glass. Here, broad strokes of thin colour are applied with round sable brushes, and the shape of the bottle is outlined.

2 Moving on to the bottle, the basic colours are blocked in. Notice how close they are to the dark background that has already been established.

3 Linear details on the bottle neck are drawn in black with the point of a fine sable brush and the initial tones are developed with fairly thick, opaque colour.

4 Working from the subject, the artist builds up the observed local colour and muted reflections of the glass. The paint here is applied carefully – each colour is blended into the neighbouring one to give the impression of a smoothly rounded glass surface.

5 The brush is dragged across the horizontal curves of the bottle neck – a technique frequently used to help create the reflective quality of very shiny surfaces such as this.

6 Before applying final details, the artist gives the painting a coat of retouching varnish to bring up the colours. Here, a broad soft brush is used, but a finer brush is more suitable for small areas.

7 When the retouching varnish is completely dry, the highlights are touched in with a fine sable brush.

8 The finished image reflects both the approach and the techniques used in the Tom Adams painting. These include working from dark to light and the use of retouching varnish to enhance the picture surface.

BELL'S WHISKY/ACRYLIC

METALLIC SURFACES

Unlike for wood and glass, there is no easy formula for painting metals. Metallic surfaces vary considerably, both in texture and colour. Some are highly reflective; others, like the tin box shown in this demonstration, have a dulled surface with no very bright highlights to lift the image.

Like the rest of the items in the Bell's advertisement, the tin box was painted from direct observation. The artist started by blocking in the main areas of colour, laying the darker tones first. These were then developed and worked with lighter colours and detail.

Notice how the rounded corners of the box in the demonstration are painted with delicately feathered strokes of light and dark greys. The more usual method of blending colours would be to work the edges of the joined colours together with water. But that would have created a bland, smooth surface and the artist wanted to emphasize the specific character and texture of tin. The feathered cross-hatching technique offered a more effective means of doing this.

Colour is all important when depicting metal. The tin box was painted in various tones of grey mixed mainly from black and white, with occasional touches of added colour to emphasize how light falls on it. Copper, gold, brass and pewter have similar surface qualities to tin, yet they are all easily recognizable by their distinctive and very different colours. For the artist it is important to depict these colours accurately – it is frequently the most effective way of emphasizing a particular type of metal.

FAR RIGHT *The first full section of the painting, with part of the second, showing Tom Adams' masterly treatment of the different textures of wood, glass, metal and leather.*

Metallic surfaces

1 General areas of light and shade are blocked in first. These are established loosely and will be modified as the image develops.
2 The artist works into the initial underpainting, strengthening the tones with thicker, more opaque paint. Painting directly from the subject, a touch of observed yellowish grey is added to the inside of the box.
3 Working with a very fine sable brush, the artist blends the light and dark areas together. The crude joins of the initial blocking in are disguised with overlaid, feathery brushstrokes.
4 Dark lines are used to emphasize the cut-out metal shapes. Working from direct observation, the details of the inside of the box are painted in.
5 The artist refines the rounded corners after the background is established as approximate areas of thin colour. The background gives a three-dimensional feeling to the box – further helped by the small shadow, which follows the edge of the shelf.
6 Before adding final details, the artist gives the painting a coat of retouching varnish.

BELL'S WHISKY/THE TECHNIQUES

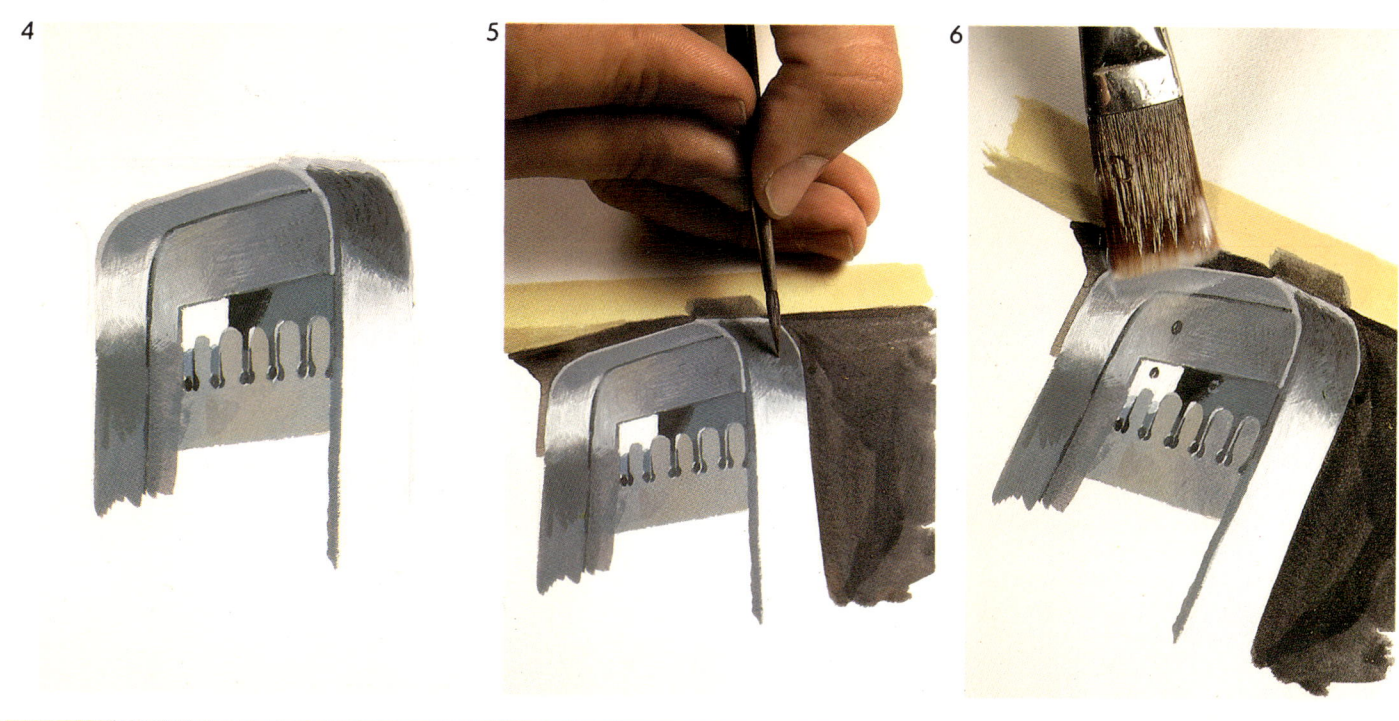

4

5

6

47

OCÉ/THE CLIENT BRIEF

The front cover of the zebra brochure — a close-up of the inside illustration. The enlargement demonstrates the artist's ability to paint fine detail.

THE CLIENT	OCÉ
THE BRIEF	TO INCREASE OCE'S SHARE OF THE PHOTOCOPIER MARKET, AND ESTABLISH A DEFINED CUSTOMER BASE
THE AGENCY	ADVANCED BUSINESS CONCEPTS
DESIGN GROUP	HAPPY DAY DESIGN
ART DIRECTORS	LEEN LOEF AND MARTIN ENGELAAN
COPYWRITER	RONALD MOL
ARTIST	MARCEL ROZENBURG

Océ.ZekerOnderscheid.

This campaign is designed to promote the product through a sophisticated use of illustration, using a mailing shot and a follow-up gift. It is a two-stage programme.

First, a leaflet with a reply card is sent out to 5000 targeted companies that may be interested in the client's product — Océ photocopiers. As the mailing is aimed at a knowledgeable audience, the copy is detailed and technical. The front cover of each leaflet — there are four in the series — features an enlarged detail of a painting shown in full on the inside. By returning the reply card sent with the leaflet the customer will receive a full-size, high-quality print of the painting with Océ's name and logo featured — although very subtley. And, of course, if there is a good response, then Océ will have a useful list of interested potential customers. The illustrations used in a campaign such as this must be of sufficient calibre to tempt customers to respond. They have to be comparable to a fine-art, limited edition print.

The main copy lines show a simple but clever connection between the imagery and the product: the cheetah title translates as 'beautifully quick', the elephant as 'reliability', and the giraffe as 'high worker', emphasizing the product's ability to cope with a high stack of paper. The zebra featured in the subsequent pages is about high-quality definition.

The enlarged details clearly show the standard of the artist's work — virtually every individual hair is painted in. The paintings demonstrate a detailed knowledge of acrylic-painting techniques. And they required patience and careful attention to detail! Although Marcel Rozenburg needed only 10 days to complete each one, he worked a 12-hour day.

The finished image of the zebra. This was reproduced as a high-quality print to be given away to potential customers.

OCÉ/THE ROUGHS

Interview with Leen Loef and Martin Engelaan

DICK WARD What was your original brief?
LEEN LOEF We were briefed to create a mailing shot that would test response and help to define a market for Océ photocopiers.
DW What was the timing?
MARTIN ENGELAAN About two months. It wasn't a lot of time, but Marcel worked very hard.
DW How does the campaign work?
LL It's a mailer, designed in two stages with leaflet and return card in the first part and a superb print of the illustration in the second. The front cover of the leaflet has an enlarged section of the inside illustration, which is virtually unrecognizable – deliberately. The idea is to make the recipient open it out of curiosity – be drawn in by the complete illustration and then read the copy which is mainly technical information – apart from the phonetic in the cheetah poster that suggests running.
DW Did you do the rough drawings?
LL Martin and I worked on them together. There are four different leaflets – the cheetah, the giraffe, the elephant and the zebra.
ME When the customer sends in the reply card, the sales person who makes the follow-up will give him or her the poster as an introduction.
LL We hope that people will want the prints – they are so good – and maybe hang them on the wall.
DW Is the idea to get a response you can measure?
LL Yes. We want to narrow down the potential customers and also maintain Océ's publicity in a sophisticated way.
DW Do you think it's a constructive use of illustration?
ME Yes. We felt we had a good product and wanted to reflect that quality. Marcel Rozenburg's work can stand on its own in any art gallery, and the posters are well printed, so we're expecting a good response.
DW Why did you choose illustration

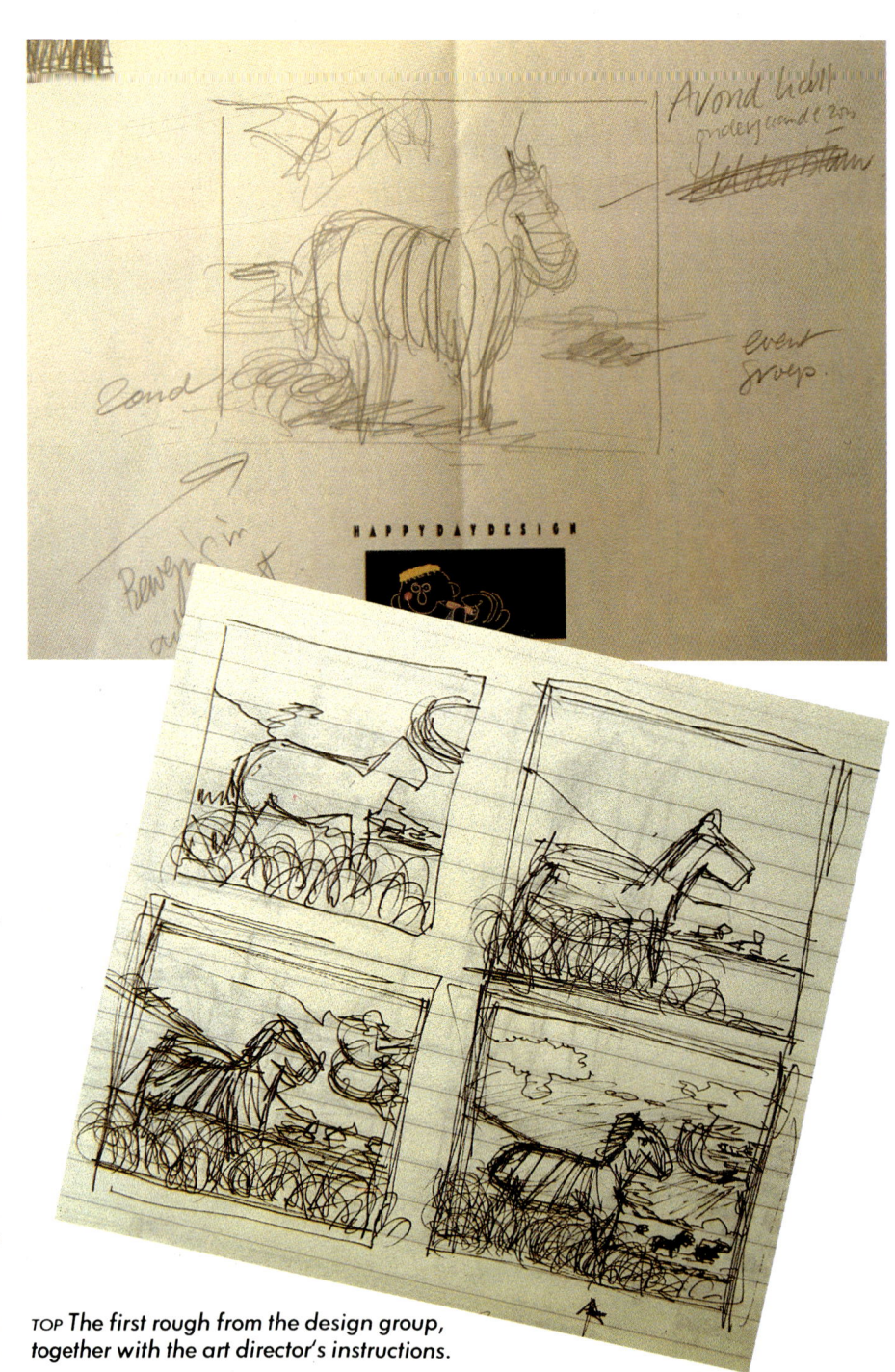

TOP **The first rough from the design group, together with the art director's instructions.**

ABOVE **Marcel Rozenburg's first roughs – merely scribbles to work out the preliminary composition.**

RIGHT **A selection of reference material used by the artist.**

OCÉ/THE ROUGHS

The finished trace ready to be transferred on to the prepared mahogany. The artist adds the zebra stripes after the outline is traced down on to the board.

INSET *The reference photograph for the zebra — the pose of the one on the left is repeated in the picture.*

instead of photography?
LL To use photography for this kind of campaign would have been wrong. A photograph is always a photograph, nothing changes. It's different with a good painting. The more you look at it the more there is to see. Wild animals are also very beautiful and Marcel's paintings show this and make them come to life.
DW How did you hear of the artist?
LL We have known of him for sometime and watched his work develop over the years.

Interview with Marcel Rozenburg

DICK WARD What's your method of constructing a painting like this?
MARCEL ROZENBURG I work from the background to the foreground. In this case the setting sun and the clouds were

51

OCÉ/THE ARTIST

put in first, and then the landscape with the small zebras. Then I did the grass and, finally, the zebra in the foreground.
DW Three of the illustrations show movement. Was this your idea?
MR That started with the cheetah, the first one I did. The copy starts with 'Tjabaf, Tjabaf, Tjabaf' – phonetic language to suggest the sound of the cheetah running. On the other paintings I made the animal just flick its tail or paw the ground. It helps to give life to the paintings. The only one I didn't add a little 'blur' to was the elephant, but then they don't usually move so fast!
DW Why do you always paint on wood?
MR I like a solid surface to work on and it helps to keep my originals in good shape. When I first started I used canvas but it moves up and down all the time when you put your pencil or brush on it – and I prefer a smoother surface.
DW Which wood do you use?
MR Mahogany, which is used on boats. It's very strong and doesn't warp.
DW Do you mount or batten it on the back?
MR No, it's not necessary.
DW How do you prepare it?
MR I paint over it with an acrylic base paint – about 20 times. Then I rub it down with wet sandpaper and it becomes smoother than paper. It takes a few days to create a surface similar to masonite board – which is popular in the United States – and can be bought ready-made. But I prefer to prepare my own surface.
DW Do you prepare a lot of panels in advance?
MR Yes, if I know I have a job coming and I know the size of it, I'll get the wood ready.
DW Where did you find your reference?
MR I went to the zoo and took some pictures.
DW How long did each illustration take?
MR About 10 days for each one. I work at home in the evenings as well as all day in the studio. It's a 12-hour day when I have a job like this on.
DW How do you begin the painting?
MR I trace the sketch down on the board,

Océ.HoogWerker.

Océ.HoogWerker.

OCÉ/THE ARTIST

LEFT *The giraffe print and the front cover of the brochure showing a detail of the animal's hide.*

ABOVE *The cheetah print – the blur on the legs is the normal way to suggest speed, and the artist has added the streaked sky to enhance the effect.*

LEFT *The art director's visual for the Cheetah brochure.*

BELOW *The elephant print – note the beautiful finish and the slight shimmering effect above the animal that suggests heat.*

and then go over the whole board with a light neutral colour, grey or sepia, so that I have no white left; I put this on with a small roller. It is the same method the Renaissance painters used.

DW What is the purpose of this neutral coat? Do you cover the whole board with a neutral tone even if you're going to paint, say, a light blue sky?

MR Yes. It means I don't have to paint the white away – it's simpler to tone it down before I start to paint. Here I've used a light grey. It gives me a more solid colour and it's easier to paint.

DW Then you paint in the background?

MR Yes. I masked the foreground zebra with adhesive film before I sprayed the background.

DW You use an airbrush?

MR I used it on the sky for speed – to get the same effect by painting can take hours. The rest is painted by hand.

DW How do you achieve the fine detail – such as on the blades of grass or the zebra's coat?

MR I use very small brushes, standard sizes 0 to 3, and I prefer brushes with a ferrule that's exactly the same width as the brush thickness.

DW Did you have reference for the grass?

MR No. That is more of a feeling.

DW How do you paint the zebra?

MR First I paint it in pale grey, then add the black stripes and finally I finish with the fine white hairs.

DW Do you use retouching varnish?

MR No. I only use a matt varnish at the end of the painting, then if a correction is necessary it's still possible to work over it. In any case, a gloss varnish can create problems when a slide is made.

DW Is the close-up a separate painting?

MR No, it's an enlargement from the original painting.

DW What medium do you use – water or acrylic?

MR I only use water. I tried retarders once but they didn't work for me.

DW What are retarders supposed to do?

MR Slow down the drying process, to give the same effect as oil paints. But I think my paintings look like oils anyway.

OCÉ/ACRYLIC

It is quite rare for commercial artists to work on wood as Marcel Rozenburg does, and especially to take such painstaking care in preparing the surface. As well as being a superb painter, he uses the airbrush, seeing it, very sensibly, as a useful aid to help him paint a large area quickly. An interesting aspect of these paintings is the way the artist has portrayed movement. Before the camera was invented artists had great difficulty in painting movement, especially of animals – in nineteenth century hunting scenes the horses' legs were extended front and back. Marcel Rozenburg has used the camera for reference to paint the little touches of movement in this case – the little flicks of the tail or the leg pawing the ground would not be seen by the naked eye, but need to be captured on film.

PREPARATION

The artist chooses the smoothest pieces of mahogany possible and prepares them carefully. Cutting them to size he begins by painting with acrylic base paint. He allows each coat to dry completely before proceeding with the next one; he will give each piece of wood about 20 coats of base paint before rubbing it down with wet sandpaper. The result is a superbly smooth surface.

THE BACKGROUND

After tracing down the image, the artist uses a small roller to paint the prepared board with a neutral grey or cream, a fairly unusual step based on the idea that it is easier to build up colour on a subdued surface than a pure white one. Although some people may consider the method old-fashioned, judging by the finish that Marcel Rozenburg achieves, the method suits him. The artist also uses the airbrush, so, on the one hand, he is very traditional and, on the other, uses a very modern commercial method to save time. Many painters disdain the airbrush, or can't use it, but Marcel Rozenburg is versatile enough to use it to his advantage.

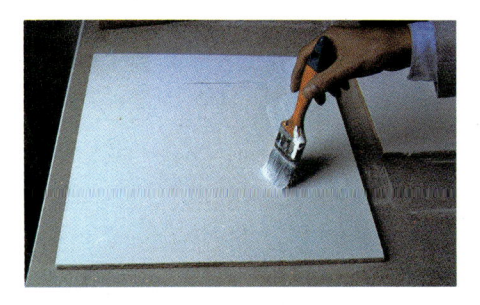

1 The mahogany is painted with acrylic base paint – this is the first of many coats, before the wood is rubbed down with wet sandpaper.

2 The image is traced on to the smooth wooden surface.

3 The neutral colour is rolled over the traced down image. This makes it easier to achieve stronger colours quickly.

4 The zebra is masked out with adhesive film, and the base colour of the sunset in the background and the grey foreground is airbrushed in.

5 The masking film removed to expose the zebra in the foreground – now ready for final detail.

6 The clouds and background details are painted first, then the black stripes on the zebra.

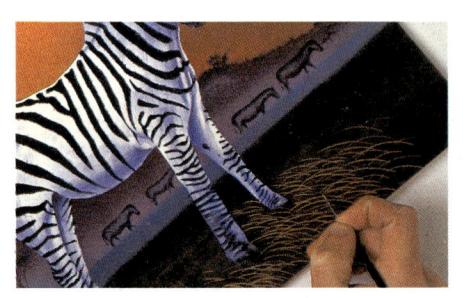

7 The grass is painted in using a palette of very similar colours that help to slowly build up depth and perspective.

8 The artist then starts painting the hairs on the zebra. The texture is added over the whole animal and the outline will be softened as well.

OCÉ/THE TECHNIQUES

THE DETAIL

The artist uses very small brushes, from standard size 0 to 3, to achieve the fine detail in his work. This is a matter of personal taste, of course; many painters use a standard, long-haired no 3 for even the finest detail, as it can be used to achieve a thin line and has the advantage of holding more paint. But Marcel Rozenburg's method is vindicated by the incredible detail in the finish of the paintings.

TOP *The finished painting of the zebra. The superb technique and the amount of detail the artist puts in to his work is obvious.*

LEFT *The image as it appears inside the brochure.*

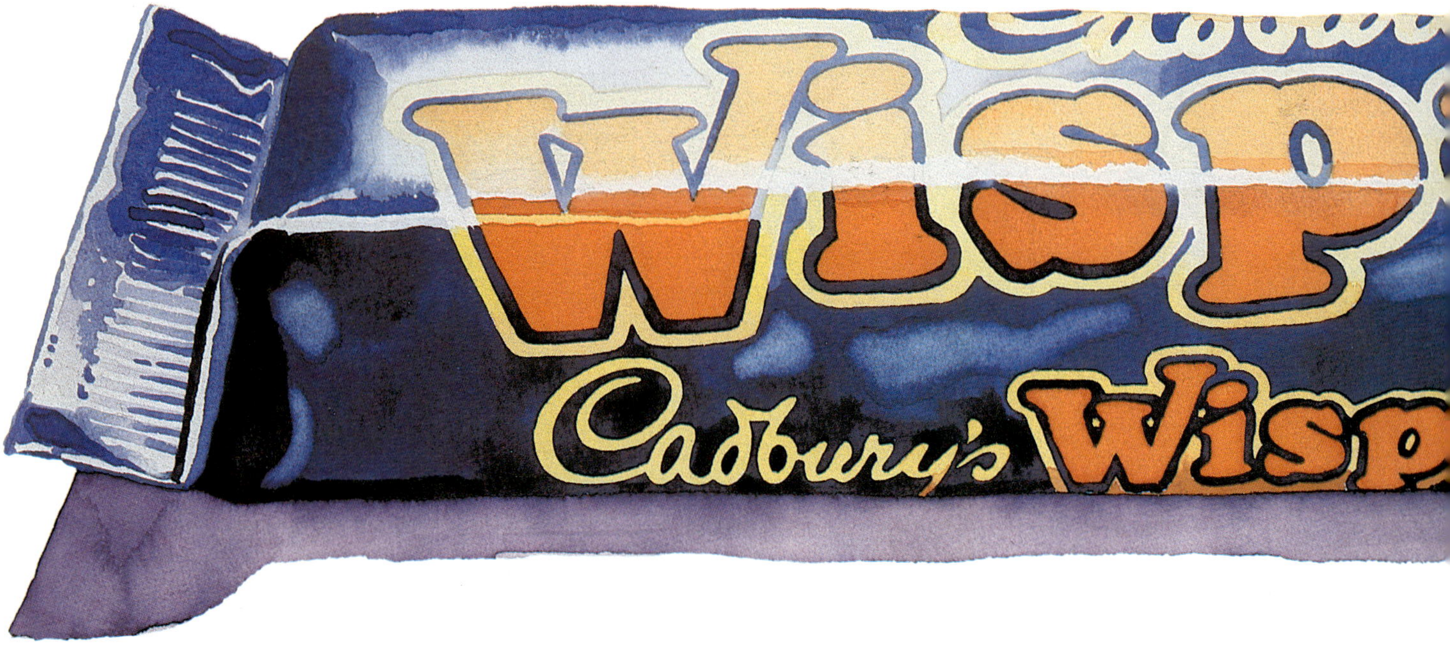
Wisp
Cadbury's
Wisp

WATERCOLOUR

Watercolour still life by Paul Webb for Cadbury's.

Watercolours are made from very finely ground pigments and gum arabic – the gum dissolves in water, and the resulting mixture adheres to paper when dry. There are three main pigments used: earth, organic and chemical. The latter stains the surface of the paper more than the others

Using watercolour is about 'drawing' with the paint: even the lightest pencil line may spoil the painting. Once they have applied the transparent wash, the basis of true watercolour and the single most important skill to master, most illustrators use the paint to draw the image, before adding the broader tones to complete the illustration – sometimes projecting the image directly on to the paper, but always avoiding the necessity of a pencil outline. There should be no areas of 'touching up' or pencil 'fill-in' where the wash has gone wrong.

Watercolour painting is enjoying something of a revival in commercial use. This difficult but rewarding technique has a freshness and spontaneity that is often missing from photographs or the more mechanical illustrative methods.

EVIAN /THE CLIENT BRIEF

THE CLIENT	EVIAN
THE BRIEF	TO INCREASE CONSUMER AWARENESS OF EVIAN AS A MAJOR BRAND OF MINERAL WATER
THE AGENCY	TBWA
ART DIRECTOR	JOHN KNIGHT/MALCOLM GASKIN
ARTIST	CONNY JUDE

In this long-running campaign, succeeding art directors have continued a successful format established by John Knight. It's an adventurous approach using a free and confident watercolour style.

When mineral water first became popular, it was bought mainly by higher income groups. Now a much wider consumer base has been established, as the progression of this campaign clearly demonstrates. The first poster (billboard) features a fit-looking, young woman who drinks Evian mineral water as part of her daily fitness regime. Five years on, the same woman is a little older and has a child, but is still extremely active: she drinks the product not only to keep in shape but because she likes it. The copy lines also reflect this change of emphasis, from fitness – 'in the pink' – to good, old-fashioned purity – 'natural mountain spring water' – which underlines the idea that to many people it tastes better than tap water.

Conny Jude is the perfect illustrator for a campaign of this nature: her style, with its fresh, spontaneous appeal, reflects the product in a far more positive fashion than a photograph of a bottle or of a joyful woman by a mountain stream would have done. The imaginative decision of art director John Knight to use this artist in an untried medium has been vindicated by the campaign's success in placing Evian among the brand leaders.

Interview with John Knight and Malcolm Gaskin

DICK WARD What made you think of this approach initially, John?
JOHN KNIGHT Ordinary photographs had been running with nice copy lines on them. I felt the campaign needed a fresh approach, and it seemed logical to use watercolour as we're selling water! So I decided to use pink and blue, the colours on the label, with the copy line 'in the pink', which conveys the idea that mineral water is good for you. But then

EVIAN/THE CLIENT BRIEF

ountain spring water

evian®

u minérale naturelle

we received an objection to the copy line, so when the budget increased the following year to enable us to do 48-sheet posters, we left the word 'pink' off and just said 'keeps you in the...'
DW Was this the first ad that Conny Jude did?

JK Yes. Her style seemed perfect for the campaign. We didn't want a lot of copy on it, as it was going on the street as well as the underground (subway), and you can't read very much when driving past a poster. We already had the pink and blue and the idea of watercolour, which looks

*The finished image – **ready to go on street and underground (subway) station sites**.*

EVIAN /THE CLIENT BRIEF

bright and fresh. We had to find a way of getting the health idea over – we decided on a bus stop, with a line of people looking depressed, their heads down, and a young woman running by 'in the pink'!
I wanted it to appeal to women as they do most of the shopping, so a fashion-orientated illustration, rather than a male-orientated one, seemed right. That's when we decided to use Conny Jude, even though she'd never worked in watercolour before! But I persuaded her to have a go, and now almost all of her work is watercolour.
DW What about the lettering? Did she do that from the beginning?
JK Yes, but the words have changed. We weren't convinced people understood that the word pink should be there.
DW What was your latest brief, Malcolm?
MG To maintain the image of healthy living but less overtly than before. You don't have to be out jogging all the time to be healthy.
DW You didn't want to change the artist or style of the campaign?
MG No, I think Conny Jude's style is perfect for this product. There's no big, heavy-selling message and she has a light and fresh approach.
DW Have you succeeded in broadening the market?
MG Yes, people always drank bottled water abroad, but it's a comparatively recent development in Britain and in the USA. Now it's spreading all over the country and to most economic groups. And Evian is the most popular still water. The whole campaign has worked extremely well.

ABOVE **The art director's rough; the main type is the same as on the label.**

RIGHT **Conny Jude's early work using crayon. Her drawing ability appealed to the art director, who was confident she could use watercolour.**

FAR RIGHT **The 'bus stop' poster (billboard), the first of the campaign. Conny Jude spent time sketching people as they waited for buses.**

EVIAN/THE ARTIST

Interview with Conny Jude

DICK WARD How did you get this job?
CONNY JUDE I did the first Evian drawing about five years ago and I suppose that was my big break. I'd been freelancing for about four years then, and it was my first major campaign.
DW How did they hear of you?
CJ John Knight, the first art director, had seen my work and liked the style.
DW What was your brief for the latest poster?
CJ The agency sends me a rough – they're usually very rough roughs – and then I just do it in my style. This particular one is of a mother running after her child. They're changing the image of the Evian woman. At the beginning of the campaign she looked super fit, someone who did aerobics and worked out, but after five years that has become a bit dated. Now the idea is to get people to feel they don't have to spend hours in a gym before they can enjoy a glass of Evian. It's appealing to an older, or at least a wider, market.
DW What's your timing on the job?
CJ Not long, usually about a week.
DW Is that from when you get the first roughs from the agency?
CJ Yes. I take about four days to do some working traces, with the rest of the time on the finished art, which isn't that

61

EVIAN/THE WORKING TRACES

ABOVE The working trace for the main heading.

RIGHT The working trace for the main figure is a good drawing in itself. Conny Jude projects this trace onto the paper using a large light box — thereby avoiding pencil lines on the finished painting.

BELOW Two other examples of Conny Jude's work from previous campaigns, showing the progression of the central figure.

62

EVIAN/THE WORKING TRACES

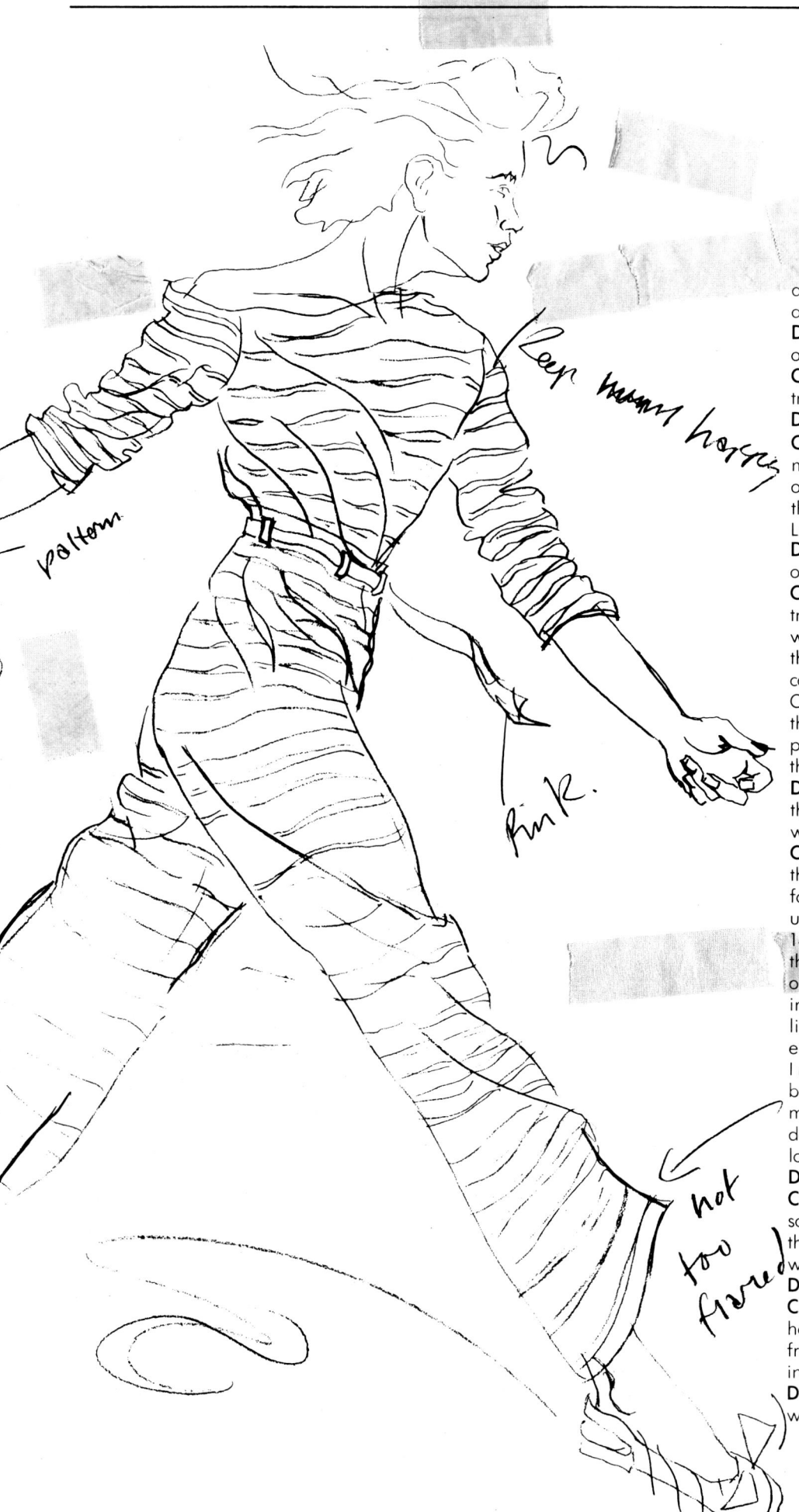

different from the rough except in size and finish.
DW Do you make a start with a pencil outline?
CJ I do lots of very big pencil sketches on tracing paper.
DW Do you trace down in the normal way?
CJ No. I use a very large light box – I put my tracing on it with the drawing paper over the top and the image shows through. I use a copyscanner (Camera Lucida) just to check proportions.
DW That's why there are no pencil lines on the finished art.
CJ Yes. I do all the preliminary work on tracing paper and, when I'm satisfied with the pencil outline, I usually cut up the tracing to get movement into the composition and into the figures.
On this campaign I did the figures and the background separately, and the printers put them together. I just gave them a position guide.
DW As you don't have a pencil line on the actual painting, you're drawing with water.
CJ That's right. It's the only way to keep the freedom and spontaneity. I do the face first and if I get that wrong I tear it up and start again. I might end up doing 14 or 15 faces before it's right, and then the rest just tends to flow. It's strange, but once I put the mark down I know immediately if it's wrong, even just a top lip or something as small, with nothing else around it.
I mix all my paint first and have it ready, because you can't start re-mixing in the middle of a wash. The actual painting doesn't always take very long, but I do a lot of preparation beforehand.
DW What materials do you use?
CJ Watercolour and gouache. And sometimes very strong water-based inks that dye the paper, which I then dilute with bleach and draw on it.
DW You've achieved a very free style.
CJ I might do 20 drawings to get that. I have to work constantly to keep the freedom in a painting and I know instantly when it's not working.
DW How long have you been using watercolour?

EVIAN/THE ROUGHS

Part of the finished illustration – actual size of the original. Most artists who use watercolour tend to work as large as possible.

64

EVIAN/THE ROUGHS

TOP Conny Jude takes black and white prints from the finished painting and assembles them to make a position guide for the printer.

ABOVE The artist's rough. Conny Jude regards this as a dress rehearsal for the finished image; there is very little difference apart from size.

CJ I hate to admit it, but the Evian campaign was the first time!
DW What did you use before?
CJ Crayon, but watercolour has opened me up to brush strokes, I really enjoy using it. Crayons are just for tidying up and putting in the extra highlights now.
DW What paper do you work on?
CJ Bockingford watercolour.
DW Do you mount it?
CJ No. It's very heavy so I just attach it at the top with double-sided tape.
DW Doesn't it curl up?
CJ I don't wet it too much so that doesn't happen. I tend to do the delicate parts with a small brush, and use a big brush and a lot of water on the large areas. I wet the area to be covered and dribble the paint into it so it bleeds. Then I mop up the colour – not the paint – with a tissue. I use the edge of a tissue on the edge of the colour, and then the water soaks into the tissue allowing the paint to dry naturally so there's no nasty hard mark left.
DW Do you ever blot it on the top?
CJ No, unless I've gone horribly wrong. But then it's normally too late to save it, so I'd throw it away and start again.
DW Is there any way of covering up an error?
CJ Not really, unless you make a pattern out of it! Which can be done sometimes.
DW Do you ever use masking fluid?
CJ Only to mask something out so I can draw over it, or to maintain a defined edge between overlapping objects. I tend to use a hair dryer to dry it quickly, because if I put something away for half an hour to dry I can't get going again.
DW Do you use live models or magazines for reference?
CJ Both. If I can get a friend to pose, that's marvellous, but it's not always possible, and it takes so long to set up. So I use lots of magazines, fashion ones mostly. I might take the head of one model and the body of another and the clothes of someone else, and so on. I tear the photographs out of the magazines and pin them up around me and draw from there. I check the proportions on the copyscanner (Camera Lucida), although

EVIAN/THE REFERENCE

the figures for Evian are fashion orientated with longer legs than real life.
DW You don't use a Polaroid?
CJ I find them too small. If I have background figures, as in the first illustration I did for Evian which had a bus queue, I go out and take notes and do little thumbnail sketches of people. I watch how people stand – for instance, someone might be leaning on an umbrella, or have a little dog. (I try to get my dog in the posters all the time but he often gets wiped out!)
DW Your drawings are very large. Is that to do with the size of reproduction or is it your own preference?
CJ A bit of both. If I'm asked to do a drawing that's going to be reproduced an inch (2.5cm) square I tend to do it about a foot (30cms) square. I'm getting better though, because the art director complained that they were so large he couldn't get them under the copyscanner (Camera Lucida) to do his layout! My originals are half the size they used to be.

ABOVE Some of the artist's reference material. Conny Jude pins this around her drawing board as a constant source of inspiration.

BELOW The finished ad on site showing how the watercolour retains its brightness, even after printing and enlargement.

EVIAN/THE TECHNIQUES

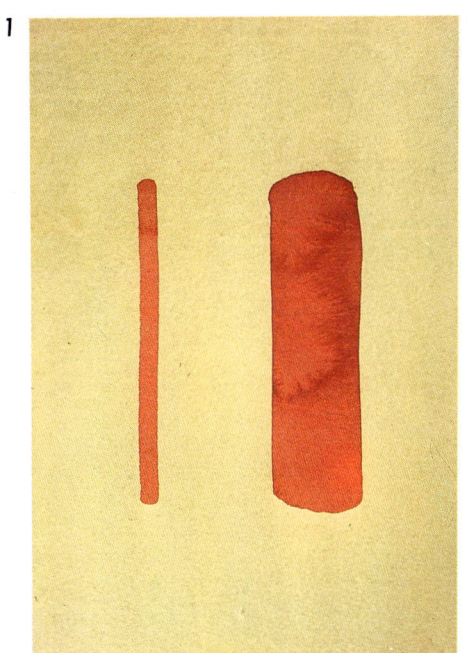

Wet on dry

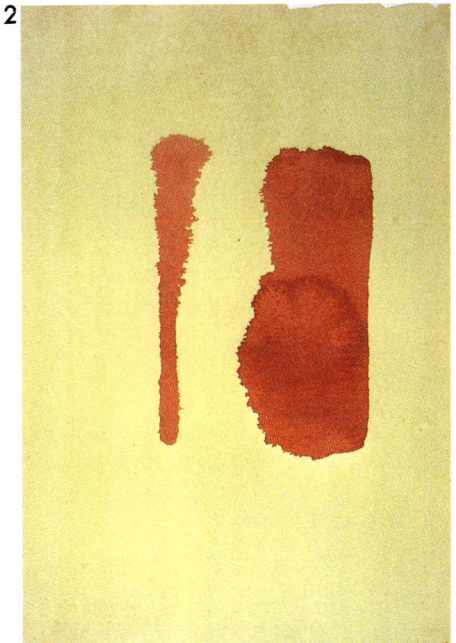

Wet on damp

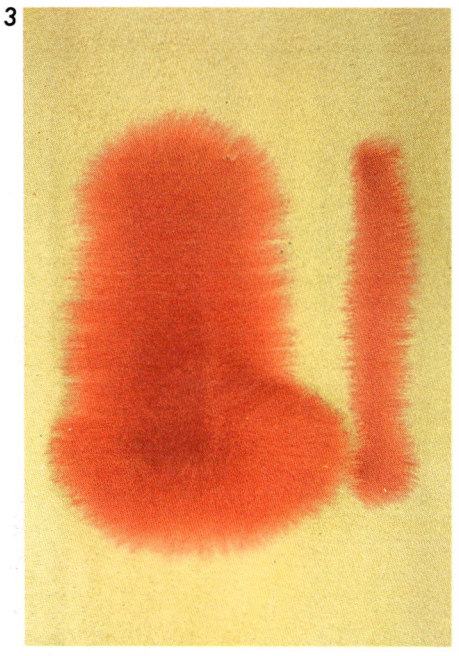

Wet on wet

Basic effects

1 Wet on dry. This method, which produces clean, crisp edges, is used for fine, detailed work. By allowing the paint to dry completely, or by working on a dry sheet of paper, the artist can retain absolute control over the brushstroke.
2 Wet on damp. The characteristic soft effect of traditional watercolour is achieved by working on slightly damp undercolour or paper. The final effect depends on the degree of dampness, but the experienced artist is able to assess this and to anticipate the result.
3 Wet on wet. Here the colours are allowed to run and bleed, producing a spontaneous yet random result. The technique is often used as a starting-off point, with the more controlled techniques used for the following stages of the work.

When Conny Jude works on a wet surface, she is using a technique known as 'wet on wet'. The support is made very wet so the colour floods into the wet area and blurs. Two other watercolour techniques are called 'wet on dry' and 'wet on damp'. Most watercolour artists, like Conny Jude, will combine all three approaches. For instance, she paints the lettering on a completely dry surface where the brushstroke holds its shape and the edges of the mark are clean and precise. If the support is slightly damp, the shape will still be recognizable but softer, depending on the degree of dampness; on a very wet support the shape will be blurred. The 'wet on wet' method is rarely used on its own for a whole illustration, because it is very difficult to control the final result, but it is frequently employed in conjunction with the tighter, 'wet on dry' approach.

Successful watercolour painting demands a high degree of patience and discipline. The paint takes time to dry, and failure to wait results in a mess which usually cannot be salvaged. To save time, an artist often works on two or three illustrations at a time, moving from one to another as drying time permits. Conny Jude solves the problem by often working in sections, and leaving the printer to assemble the final image assisted by a position guide which she supplies.

EVIAN / WATERCOLOUR

THE SUPPORT

Illustrators using watercolour work on a wide variety of surfaces, ranging from very smooth illustration boards, to coarse, hand-made specialist papers. Conny Jude uses Bockingford 140 watercolour paper, a heavyweight paper with a mid texture, 2, right. The texture of the support surface plays an important role in the appearance of the finished picture: for instance, very rough papers and boards tend to create broken lines and colour, with tiny white flecks of the pitted surface showing through; colours look flatter on smooth surfaces, and generally, watercolours lose something of their luminosity and glow if the paper is very smooth. The samples on the right demonstrate how a variety of popular supports affect watercolour.

Conny Jude tapes her paper at the top using double-sided tape: she only uses water on sections of her work, so the heavy paper she uses doesn't curl. If a less substantial paper is being used, it should be soaked and stretched on a board, and allowed to dry naturally; excessive heat causes the sheet to shrink and tear. The paper should remain taped to the board until the finished work is dry.

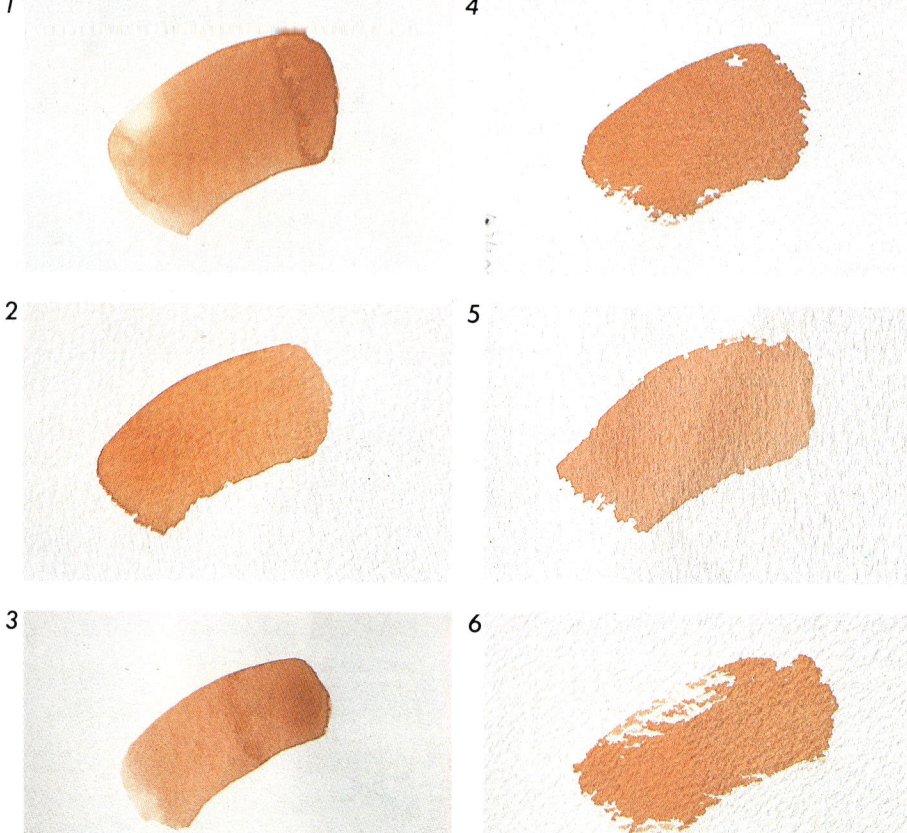

The surface texture of the paper has a decided effect on colours.
These samples show how a colour is affected by various supports. Illustrators choose paper which suits their style: Conny Jude works on mid-textured paper which allows her to use broad brushstokes with freedom.

1 Daler line board
This is a smooth, standard line board, part china clay and part synthetic, which is ironed.
2 Bockingford 140
An acid-free, rough-finish paper, made from rags. The 140 refers to the weight in pounds used to stretch the paper.
3 Saunders smooth
A pure rag paper that starts life as a rough paper, then is pressed smooth.
4 Whatman not 140
The 'not' refers to not being hot pressed – a pure rag paper with a rough texture.
5 Waterford HP140
A fibrous paper pressed for a smoother surface. HP stands for hot pressed.
6 Whatman rough
A non-pressed paper with a rough texture.

EVIAN/THE TECHNIQUES

LAYING A WASH

Most amateur watercolour artists find that laying a flat wash is the most frustrating problem they encounter. Yet it is not really difficult, and is the single most important technique of all.

A successful wash depends on several things, the most crucial of which is a good-quality paper, the heavier the better.

'Dry' washes are applied to a dry support, 'wet' washes, as the name suggests, are painted onto a dampened sheet of paper. Both can be applied as flat colour to obtain an even, overall tint, or they can be graded so the colour changes from dark to light. Wet or dry, the top of the board must be raised a little to prevent the colour from running back into the washed area.

When laying a wash, it is essential to work quickly, from the top. The bottom edge of the line of colour must be kept moving otherwise the paint starts to dry and leaves a tide mark. In the method shown here, rows of vertical and horizontal strokes are alternated; another method is to lay the wash entirely in horizontal strokes.

The amount of colour on the brush is important: too little, and the continuity of line is broken; too much, and the colour runs down the paper, out of control. Conny Jude uses a good-quality soft-bristled wash brush to make the job easier, although many prefer a soft flat brush. Some artists abandon brushes altogether and apply the colour to damp paper with a piece of real sponge.

If a wash fails, it is wise to take Conny Jude's advice and abandon it. It is very difficult to retouch or improve an uneven colour, and trying to usually makes it worse.

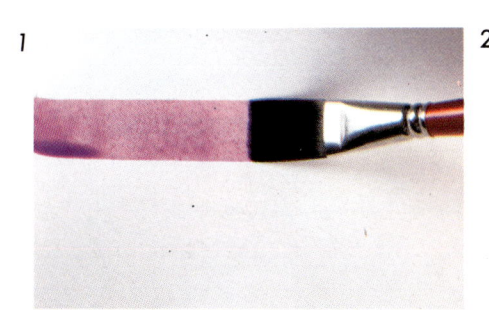

Flat wash

1 When laying a wash, tilt the board at a slight angle. Take a tip from Conny Jude and be sure to mix enough colour to cover the required area before starting to work – you need to work fast and there is no time to stop halfway through and mix more paint. Any hesitation and the paint dries in uneven tide marks. Most professionals use a flat-headed brush to lay the colour. There should be enough colour on the brush to spread evenly but not so much that the paint runs. Working quickly, a broad horizontal stroke of colour is painted across the top of the wash area.

2 It is important to keep the paint moving, spreading it quickly across the paper. To ensure an even colour, alternate horizontal strokes with vertical ones.

3 The wash is continued across the required area. Any excess paint is mopped up with tissue or a squeezed-out brush.

Graded wash

1 For a graded wash, first dampen the paper with a wet sponge. For this reason it is best to use a heavyweight paper, otherwise, tape the paper to a board. Prepare enough colour to cover the whole area and have a container of clean water close by.

2 Working in broad horizontal strokes, lay the colour with a flat wash brush. As with the flat wash, keep the colour moving continuously to prevent the edge of the paint from drying or staining the paper. Add a little water after each horizontal stroke to achieve the graded effect.

EVIAN/WATERCOLOUR

TONE

Unlike oils, acrylics and gouache, watercolour is not opaque. It has little covering or hiding power, and this makes it impossible to obliterate a dark or bright colour by painting a lighter one on top of it. Thus, the transparency of watercolour (one of its most attractive qualities) is also rather restricting.

For the illustrator who works in watercolour, it is essential to plan the stages of the work before starting to paint. The very lightest tones must be laid first, and the deeper tones added gradually so the colours get progressively darker. If the work is being done on white paper, highlights and other white areas must be left unpainted. Conny Jude's originals are a good example of this. She uses the white support as an integral part of the painting, thereby maintaining its freshness and spontaneity.

Mistakes are not always irreversible. White gouache or poster paint can be used at any stage to hide small errors and to make late, light additions. But a large area which has been painted too dark too quickly is not easy to put right. Small areas of white can sometimes be 'recreated'. If the colour is still wet, a dry brush or absorbent tissue (as the artist favours here), can be used to absorb the colour, although certain strong colours may resist and leave stains. Conny Jude sometimes uses bleach diluted with water to remove stubborn colour so that she can draw back in. It is also possible on some papers to scratch back to white using fine sandpaper or a fine knife.

The transparency of the paint means that pencil lines will show through in the finished work. In this case, the artist uses a light box to shine her image through on to the paper, thereby avoiding this problem. If a pencil line must be used it is important to keep it as light as possible and never to paint over it because then it cannot be erased without spoiling the surface of the paper.

Dry brush

Texture can be achieved in a watercolour painting by using a method known as dry brush. If you look at the Evian paintings closely, it is possible to see areas where the lines break up: in the patterns on the central figure, for example, or in some of the little flicks that give the paintings movement and help identify Conny Jude's style.

A dry-brush effect is achieved by wiping or squeezing excess paint from the bristles before brushing it across the paper. A variety of textures can be created using this technique. Here, the artist is using short, feathery, criss-cross strokes to make an overall texture, but the marks can be varied to produce different effects. The texture of the paper and the type of brush also affect the result.

Building up tone

In this example from Conny Jude's painting, the lightest tones are painted first. Here, a wash of diluted pink is laid to establish the shape of the image. When the initial wash is dry, the second lightest tone – mid-pink – is painted over the paler tone. Finally, the darkest tone – a deeper red – is added on the shadow side of the figure.

EVIAN/THE TECHNIQUES

Brush-and-ruler

On the Evian illustrations, Conny Jude uses a brush-ruling technique to hand letter the brand name. This is a very valuable skill to acquire and is an extremely useful way to create free but straight lines. If a ruling pen were used on the Evian lettering, not only would the final result look too stiff and out of context with the style of the illustration, a line would be left at the edge of the letter since the paint dries quickly.

In practice, precise straight lines are rarely painted with a brush. However, the brush and ruler technique is often employed to paint a straight edge before filling in the rest of the form, especially if a free style, such as that used for the Evian campaign, is required. When using watercolour, it is essential to work quickly because the shape must be filled in while the outline is still wet, then the filled-in colours will blend in with the brush-ruled outline to give a flat tone. The ruler is used as a guide only. Conny Jude uses a heavyweight steel ruler to give a firm support, running the ferrule of the brush along the edge of the ruler, which is held well above the paper.

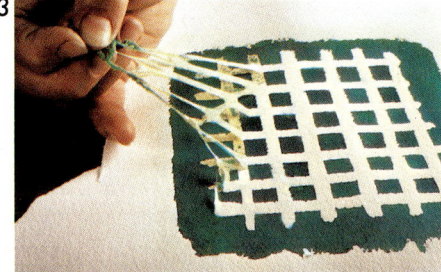

1 Using an old brush, paint the required shape in masking fluid.
2 Then apply a wash of colour over the dried masking fluid and allow this to dry.
3 Pull the dried masking fluid off gently.
4 The masked lines are revealed, and are either left white or receive further colour.

MASKING

Conny Jude uses masking fluid in her work occasionally, especially when a figure or some lettering overlaps something else and it's important to maintain a defined edge. An example of this can be seen in one of the earlier images featuring the little dog. Where the dog's lead crossed the lettering, masking fluid was used to keep the thin line. The alternative would have been to paint white gouache or poster paint over the lettering which could have resulted in a mess.

Masking fluid is rather like liquid rubber (rubber cement) and is painted onto the areas that need to remain white. Once it has dried, the area is painted and then the mask is peeled off to reveal the clean, white shape beneath. Masking fluid can be removed with an eraser or a finger but should be done cautiously — harsh rubbing on thin or cheap paper will lift off the paper surface and the surrounding paint.

Masking fluid ruins paint brushes, especially soft and sable ones, so it is best to keep an old one for the purpose. If the brushstrokes are quite loose, the negative shapes left when the fluid is removed will retain this sense of spontaneity. In this example, the masking fluid is removed by hand.

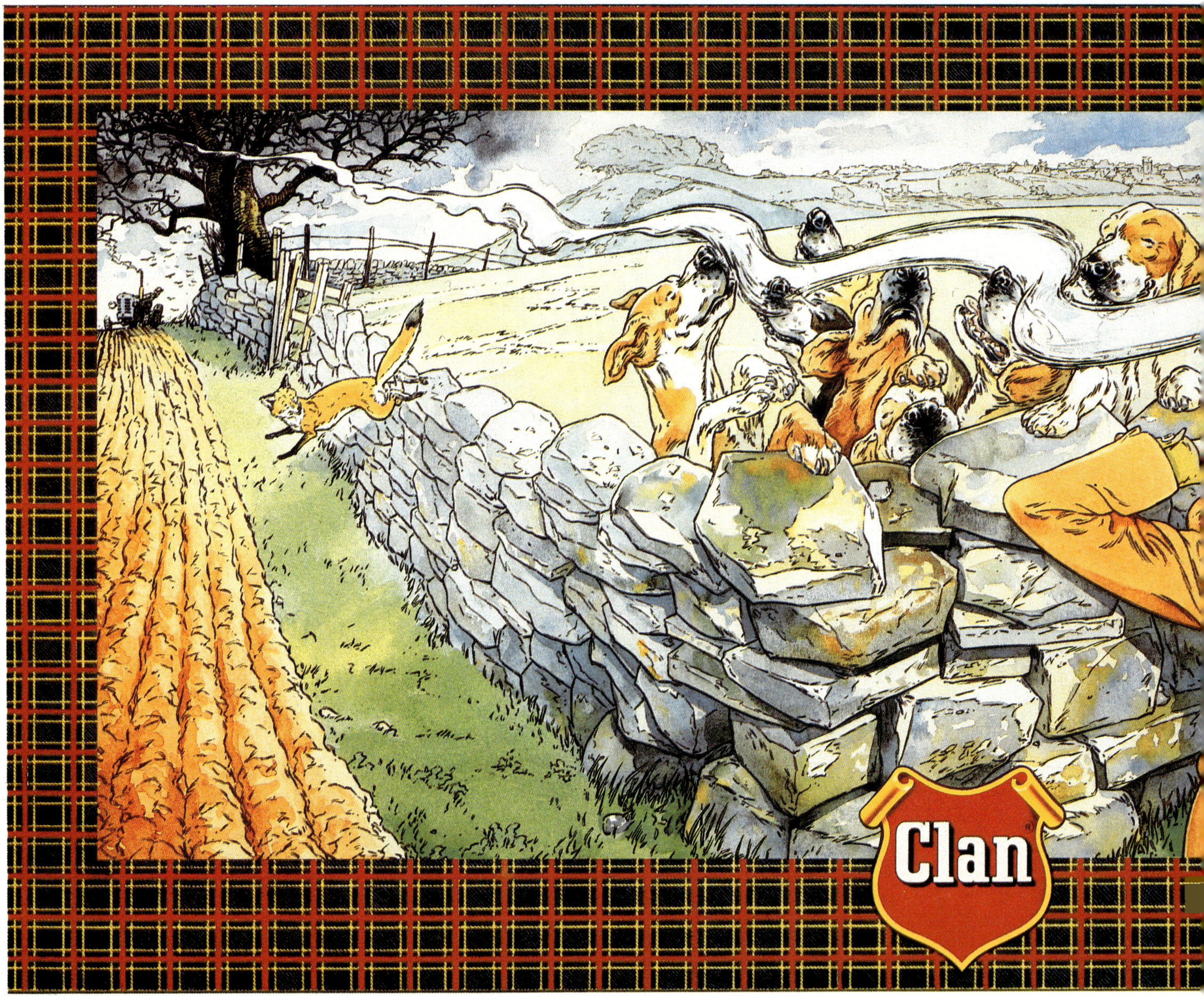
Clan

LINE AND WASH

Pen and ink drawings were the speciality of the medieval monks who illuminated manuscripts and perfected the art of calligraphy. Line combined with a wash is a technique dating back almost as far and is the logical extension of a pure line drawing. Today, a variety of techniques are used, with some artists laying a wash first and then drawing the line work or, as is more common, the line drawing is followed by a wash. The materials are traditionally Indian ink for the line work, usually drawn with a mapping pen (steel crow quill) or, for a tighter finish, with a technical pen. The wash is commonly watercolour, but sometimes inks are used for a brighter finish. Occasionally, the artist will produce two drawings – one in line and one in tone – and the printer will combine them for the finished result, although these days it is more common for one piece of artwork to be produced.

Line and wash painting by David Franklyn for Clan Tobacco.

WINES FROM SPAIN/THE CLIENT BRIEF

THE CLIENT	WINES FROM SPAIN
THE BRIEF	TO UPGRADE THE IMAGE OF SPANISH WINE, AND TO INCREASE CONSUMER AWARENESS OF THE PRODUCT
THE AGENCY	SAATCHI AND SAATCHI
ART DIRECTOR	ROGER CAZEMAGE
COPYWRITER	CHRIS BROWNE
ARTIST	MURRAY ZANONI

In this highly successful campaign, the art director chose an artist with classic technical skills, who conveys atmosphere in his paintings. In the street scene in Valencia, for instance, Murray Zanoni has cleverly faded the washes so that the viewer can imagine walking down the city street in the morning shadows, creating a distinctive southern Mediterranean impression. Roger Cazemage, art director, and Chris Browne, the copywriter, are really enjoying this campaign and it shows.

It has been very well thought-out, from establishing the mood and the imagery in the early stages to the more targeted approach in the later ads, which are more closely identified with the product. The image of Spanish wine was not a good one, and the idea of *sangria* and rough wine was difficult to change. However, the campaign has succeeded in altering this image, resulting in substantially higher sales and increasing awareness on the retail side. It is both informative and educational, and is awakening a large amount of consumer interest in the hitherto unknown qualities of the product. And a side-effect of this campaign is that the hundreds of thousands of tourists who pack Spain each summer are becoming more and more interested in the culture and the products of the country.

Interview with Roger Cazemage and Chris Browne

ROGER CAZEMAGE The campaign started about three years ago with the aim of changing the image of Spanish wines. We had to steer well clear of the rough wine and *sangria* feel to counter the negative image built up by all the cheap holidays to Spain on offer.
CHRIS BROWNE We started thinking of nice ways of drinking wine, and the more romantic imagery of Spain.
DICK WARD How did you hear about Murray Zanoni?
RC We saw his work in one of the illustration annuals – there was a good sample of North Africa and also one of Spain.
CB We were excited because his work seemed to capture the atmosphere of the Spanish interior – the unspoilt villages, the calm – which isn't so well known.
DW Had Murray done much advertising work before?

RC No. He'd done a lot of publishing work and personal work in Spain and around the world, but he hadn't been used in a major press campaign before.
DW Did the television commercial come first?
RC Yes. Part of the original brief was to make the most effective use of the money available and TV was the best way. We showed Murray's work to the client, who loved it and then presented roughs for a 30-second commercial and an insert (brochure) for one of the Sunday colour supplements (magazines given away with newspapers).
CB The brochure was the first piece of work we did for them but it took 18 months to get the commercial off the ground.

RIGHT *The finished image which is used as a full-page ad in quality colour magazines.*

BELOW *The first brochure – setting the style for the subsequent campaign, and selling wine without a picture of a wine bottle.*

WINES FROM SPAIN/THE CLIENT BRIEF

VALENCIA

THE BRITISH DISCOVERED VALENCIA LONG AGO. NOW VALENCIAN WINES HAVE DISCOVERED BRITAIN.

VALENCIA IS A BEAUTIFUL, EXCITING AND THRIVING CITY. A CITY SET ON THE MEDITERRANEAN SHORES AND SURROUNDED BY A MOUNTAINOUS AREA, COVERED WITH A PATCHWORK OF VINEYARDS.

HERE THE WINE MAKING TRADITION DATES BACK TO PRE-ROMAN TIMES.

TODAY THOSE SKILLS ARE SUPPLEMENTED BY THE MOST MODERN TECHNOLOGY. THE RESULTS ARE GOOD QUALITY, DISTINCTIVE, YET EASY TO DRINK WINES.

YOU'LL FIND THE WHITE WINES, WHETHER DRY OR SWEET, ARE LIGHT AND FRAGRANT, WITH AN ATTRACTIVE FRESHNESS.

THE REDS ON THE OTHER HAND, ARE FULL BODIED, BUT HAVE A DELIGHTFUL WARMTH AND SOFTNESS.

ALL OF THEM ARE VERY GOOD VALUE FOR MONEY, AND READILY AVAILABLE IN YOUR SUPERMARKET OR OFF-LICENCE.

IN FACT, A MILLION CASES OF VALENCIA WINES WERE ENJOYED IN BRITAIN LAST YEAR, BRINGING A LITTLE OF THE COLOUR AND WARMTH OF THE MEDITERRANEAN LIFE TO OUR SHORES.

WINES FROM SPAIN/THE CLIENT BRIEF

DW Did you go to Spain to look for locations?
RC Yes. First of all we did a crash course, to cover as many areas as we could in about 10 days!
DW Did you take your own reference shots?
RC Murray does, but he usually went out separately.
DW What was the first ad you produced?
RC A trade ad to spell out which areas we were going to promote on TV.
DW What brief did you give Murray?
CB After our trip we plotted out some likely locations for him to visit — which he probably ignored! He's very independent and likes to go his own way, so he went off for a couple of weeks and produced the three trade ad drawings for us when he came back.
DW You didn't supply him with a rough as such?
RC We had a rough for the brochure — to present to the client. We took a stat of Murray's work in an illustration annual for the front cover, and designed the typeface. Now we rough in an image from a book or postcard because we know and the client knows how Murray draws.
DW How do you see this campaign evolving?
RC Our plan now is to bring out the character of the individual areas — on the Valencia ads we used the tiles, a particular feature of the town. Before we were doing landscapes that are characteristic of the regions, but now we're concentrating on smaller, more specific areas.
DW The early drawings didn't have any figures in them. Any reason for that?
CB The interior of Spain is mostly empty, with vast plains and mountains and little villages basking in the sun. But we're adding figures now that we are using views inside the towns and the bars.
RC The interiors of some of the bars are fascinating, and it was a chance to talk about the food, the *tapas*, laid out on the counters, and the people who make the wine — and drink it.
RC The Valencia bar is the first inside scene. The town has a very different atmosphere from the north, it's very exciting and the people are sophisticated. We wandered around trying to find locations that fitted our roughs. Eventually we found a really beautiful hilltop village near the city, overlooking the sea, and when we held up the rough,

The first trade ad which appeared full-page in the wine and spirit trade press.

TOP RIGHT Agency roughs for the Valencia illustrations sketched by art director Roger Cazemage: a coastal village (left) and the interior of a tapas bar (right).

WINES FROM SPAIN/THE CLIENT BRIEF

it fitted the layout! But we finally decided not to run with the village as it was getting away from the wine-growing area.

CB We had decided to do two ads – one interior and one street scene. Some parts of Valencia are very smart, but there are still all these *tapas* bars, which were perfect for the interior.

RC To make it obvious that the ads were about wine we used the little still lifes showing typical *tapas* dishes – calamares, some slices of the ham, prawns, and so on.

CB In our wanderings we had stumbled across a market which was completely tiled. That's when we decided to use the tiles as a banner across the top. They seem to typify the region.

ABOVE **Two coloured roughs by Murray Zanoni: different views of the same scene.**

77

WINES FROM SPAIN/THE ARTIST

ABOVE The trace for the Valencia lettering, based on a traditional typeface.

Roughs for the Valencia tiles.

BELOW The finished original of the Valencia tiles — a simple, but effective use of watercolour.

WINES FROM SPAIN /THE ARTIST

THE SPAIN JUST WAITING TO BE TASTED.

Murray Zanoni's perfect little watercolour painting for the logo above the main copy line for the campaign.

DW Why didn't you show wine in the first ads?
RC We didn't feel it was necessary. We were establishing a mood, but in the second phase of the campaign we were featuring Penedés and Navarra, and we wanted to emphasise the fact that they are important wine-producing areas, which isn't widely known.
CB Originally, we wanted to keep as much white space around Murray's scenes as possible – but we tried several layouts and eventually arrived at this format which will probably continue throughout the campaign.
RC At first we were going to include the bottles and glasses in the location illustration.
CB We trailed Murray around some little mountain villages in Penedés and Navarra clutching bottles and glasses. We'd put them on walls in front of him and say, 'try shooting that!' And Murray would look at us as if we were mad and just wander off totally ignoring us!
RC He was right, of course. When we came back and looked at all the reference shots, somewhere in the corner there would be this tiny little bottle of wine! So we incorporated the wine as a separate illustration.

DW Is the cork running on all the ads?
RC Yes. The clients wanted a logo, and although a cork isn't a terribly original idea, when Murray draws something, it looks a little bit special. It also fits in with our main copy line, which has stood the test of time – 'the Spain just waiting to be tasted.'

Interview with Murray Zanoni

DICK WARD. How did you start in the business?
MURRAY ZANONI. I trained as a graphic designer in Australia, and I also worked as a typographer for a couple of years. But I always wanted to draw for a living, so I came to England in 1972 and worked in various studios in London, really as a general artist and designer. That way I gradually got a portfolio of drawings together.
DW Did that take long?
MZ Yes, but I was determined to do the kind of work I wanted to do, rather than be an all-round graphic artist.
DW How did this style develop?
MZ I've always wanted to travel and draw – mostly I do topographical drawing – I go somewhere and come back with a traditional technique that relies a lot on draughtsmanship.
DW I've noticed you don't put figures in a lot of your work. Is there a reason for that?
MZ No, just that the first commercial work I did was mainly architectural drawings – shop fronts and buildings – so I got a bit typecast, especially with the Spanish wine series nearly all being landscapes. Most people think that's all I do – but I could show you a whole book full of figure work.
DW How did the first Spanish wine job come about?
MZ When the agency pitched for the account they showed a piece of my work that had been in one of the illustration books – and the clients liked it. They wanted to get away from the current image of Spain, and try for a somewhat more sophisticated approach, so soft landscapes seemed right. The agency had come up with the copy line – 'the Spain just waiting to be tasted' – before I started, and that was my brief.
DW I know you have to go to Spain, which is time-consuming, but how long do you spend on each drawing?
MZ It varies. The Valencia street scene took about two weeks because it has a lot of detail in it. A landscape can be done in about three days.
DW Do you actually draw on location?
MZ I do sketches for my own composition, but because of the nature of the job – there are so many people who have to approve it – I take photographs and come back and show everyone involved all the various locations. One person might like one and someone else another, but I tend to quietly influence them in the direction of the location I think is best.
DW Do you use a copy scanner (Camera Lucida)?
MZ No, never.
DW So you don't do a working trace as such, first?
MZ For me the actual act of drawing is very important. I might do a little trace sketch of a still life first, and if I have trouble with a figure that's not working out, I'll probably trace it off to correct it. That's the only time I find that I need to trace. Otherwise I rely on direct contact with the paper and a pen or wash.
DW Do you draw in pencil first?
MZ I rough out the drawing in pencil and then go straight to pen and ink. On architecture there tends to be more ink than on landscape.
DW How do you do your first wash after the ink line?
MZ Once I've plotted everything out, I'll lay the first wash, which is usually the shadows.
DW Why do you put the darks in first?
MZ In watercolour you normally work from light to dark, but I put the darks in first to give form and shape, and then lay the washes in the usual way – slowly building up the strength of tone.
DW Do you find that watercolour is a difficult medium to work with?
MZ No, but I don't work with watercolour in a traditional way – it's said, for

WINES FROM SPAIN /THE FINISHED ARTWORK

example, that to retain luminosity the maximum number of washes is about 5 – but on occasions I've used 12 or even 20. I rely on the drawing underneath more than the medium, although I'll wash off with water sometimes and lay a new wash.
DW What paper do you use?
MZ Saunders.
DW Rough or smooth?
MZ Both, not (cold pressed) and hot pressed. It's a false economy to use cheap paper as it sometimes has to take a lot of strenuous treatment.
DW Do you work with watercolour or inks and dyes?
MZ Watercolour. I like the traditional mediums and inks tend to stain the paper.
DW Do you stretch or mount the paper?
MZ I stretch it – wet it first, then stretch it.
DW What do you do if a wash is too dark? Have you found a way to reduce it?
MZ There are ways – it's possible to wash off with water or use an ink eraser, and sometimes I put an opaque wash over it.
DW What, gouache?
MZ Yes. The important thing in any drawing is to know what result you want. Usually, it's possible to invent ways around problems – it is never like step one, two and three. I take any route to arrive at the image, and the clearer the view I have about that image, the easier it is to invent ways to solve problems.
DW If you start a drawing and it begins to go wrong, do you throw it away and start again?
MZ Yes. I have about a 70 per cent success rate.
DW Do you know very quickly if it's going to go wrong?
MZ Yes. It's also uncanny how your attitude at the time can affect the outcome of a painting.
DW How do you find your locations?
MZ That's an important part of it – I get a good map to plot promising sites and then I work out where the sun will rise or be at a certain time.
DW Do you draw the figures on location?
MZ I take reference shots of figures, but

TOP Murray Zanoni only uses a working tracing for the still lifes – never on the landscapes.

ABOVE The finished watercolour of the Valencia still life.

TOP RIGHT The pencil and wash working sketch made on location to establish the composition. Note how he has raised the eye level on the finished artwork.

RIGHT The first line drawing for the finished artwork on the Valencia campaign.

WINES FROM SPAIN/THE FINISHED ARTWORK

when I come to draw from the photographs, I have to change every figure to make it convincing, because in a still photograph people often don't look as if they're moving.
DW Do you use a camera with a motor-drive?
MZ Usually, but sometimes I don't want an accurate photograph, I just want information. I started using reference shots for practical reasons only, because if I actually sat on location and did a drawing I'd probably only get one done in the whole week, and then the client might not like it. I really prefer to sit and draw something, but that can cause problems because you attract too much attention – when I was drawing in India, for example, I'd sit in the street and make a start and 5 or 10 minutes later I'd be

81

WINES FROM SPAIN/THE FINISHED ARTWORK

surrounded by people. They would even pull my drawing-board down to look at what I was doing.

DW Do you actually copy from the photographs?

MZ No. One thing about drawing from photographs is that they must be used only as a reference. If you copy or trace them you're being controlled by them and that will get you nowhere. Every drawing is constructed from scratch – in the Valencia street scene I've changed the viewpoint and the horizon line to where I want it. I've put myself a lot higher up – that's what I mean about constructing a drawing, making it go the way you want it to go.

By changing the viewpoint, it feels as if you are going into the middle of the drawing, and the viewpoint is high enough to open the foreground and lose all the clutter. Drawing in its most basic form is pure geometry – every drawing must be constructed and the perspective, light and shade has to be correctly understood.

DW Is the Valencia drawing done in the morning?

MZ The quality of the morning light seemed appropriate – the ad needed to look fresh and warm – and the slight haze is typically Mediterranean. Often I'll go back to the same spot at different times of the day and record the changes of light.

DW Is this the centre of Valencia?

MZ Yes. Behind here is the old town and the market where we found the tiles.

TOP RIGHT *The second stage of the Valencia finished artwork – Murray Zanoni puts the shadows in first to give form and shape.*

RIGHT *The third stage of the Valencia finished artwork. The second wash has been laid, building up the tone.*

WINES FROM SPAIN/THE FINISHED ARTWORK

ABOVE The fourth stage of the finished artwork. The last washes have been laid to establish the tonal values of the painting.

LEFT The Valencia interior recreates the welcoming atmosphere of a Spanish bar. It is used as a full-page ad in quality colour magazines.

FAR LEFT The Navarra ad, which is also part of the current campaign, shows a typical village of the region basking in the sun. One of the first still-life paintings to push the product to the fore.

WINES FROM SPAIN /LINE AND WASH

Murray Zanoni combines the detail of line with the immediacy of watercolour washes. Line and wash is a centuries-old technique which is still very much in use. Occasionally the line is used for emphasis of tone, but in the main, shading is built up with areas of wash. The examples shown here use waterproof ink, as this is brighter for demonstration purposes and is often used in conjunction with line work, although Murray Zanoni uses watercolour.

The support must be good-quality watercolour paper or board, and it must be stretched. Its surface must suit both the washes and the pen's nib – so it is advisable to use a smooth or medium paper.

Murray Zanoni uses a variety of dip pens, from standard size to mapping, and likes them flexible, hard and sharp. He uses a combination of the techniques known as wet on wet and wet on damp when he applies the washes (see Watercolour). Washes can be applied before the lines, in order to establish the colour, atmosphere or tonal composition. However, Murray Zanoni makes a detailed and complete line drawing, using waterproof drawing ink, before adding tone and colour with the brush.

As this artist demonstrates, lines need not merely be 'outlines'. They can be used to indicate areas of tone, to build up pattern, to indicate surface texture and to plot the internal contours or form of an object or structure. And an outline need not merely enclose a shape; it can suggest the form within that shape. If a thick line is drawn on one side, for example, and a thin line on the other, the shape will instantly become three-dimensional.

If you look carefully at Murray Zanoni's first line drawing, not only does it form the basis of the painting that is to come, it is an essential part of the structure of the finished image. The lines under some of the mouldings on the buildings are thicker than others, and some of the vertical strokes are thicker than the horizontal. This is not accidental, as it gives form to the whole drawing.

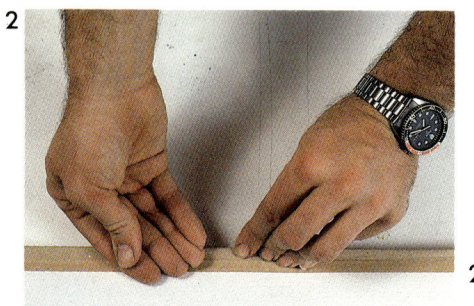

Stretching paper
1 Use a clean sponge or cloth to wet paper thoroughly before stretching. Alternatively, the sheet can be immersed in a bath or tray of water. Paper which is especially thin or lightweight tears easily and so must be handled with care.
2 Lay wet sheet on a drawing-board or other completely flat surface, right side up. Attach the sheet with brown gummed tape. The tape must be at least 1½ in (3.75cm) wide; it is important to cover both the paper edge and the surrounding board with at least ¾ in (2cm) of tape, because the paper contracts as it dries, pulling away from the tape, or causing the tape to pull away from the board.

Dip pen
1 Murray Zanoni uses a strong-nibbed dip pen on smooth or medium paper.
2 This gives a clean line without 'catching' the surface.

WINES FROM SPAIN/THE TECHNIQUES

Wet into wet
1 An alternative line and wash technique is to draw on to a wet area of colour.
2 Depending on the dampness of the wash, the lines bleed and partially merge with the surrounding colour.

Waterproof ink
Waterproof ink can be used instead of watercolour in conjunction with line work, particularly when a crisp, linear image is required.
1 The colour is washed over the paper.
2 The underlying lines still retain their sharpness.

85

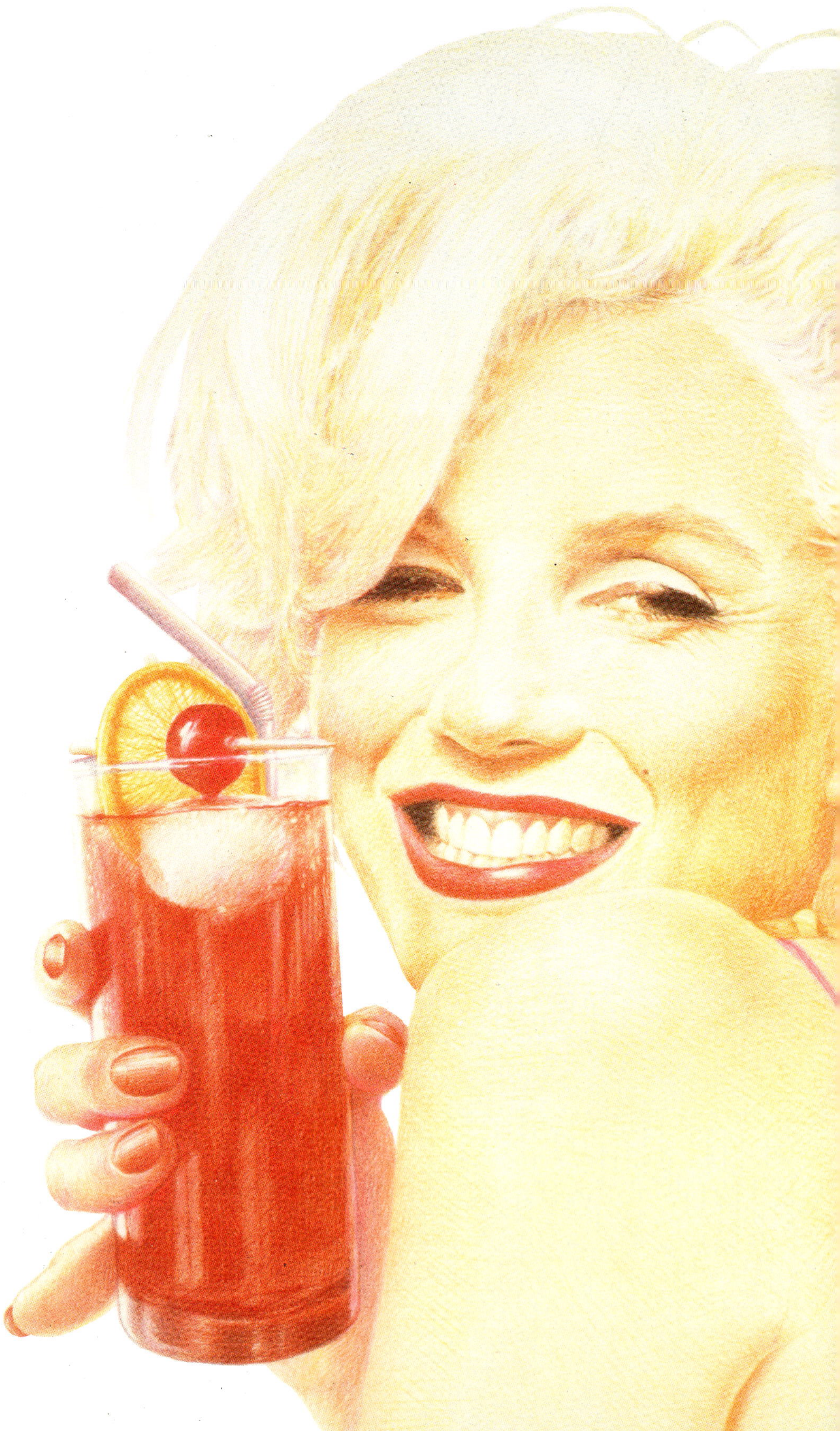

PENCIL

The humble pencil has come a long way since the crude graphite sticks that were first developed in Europe during the latter half of the seventeenth century. Within another century, Faber in Germany had developed the pencil further using a mix of one part sulphur to two parts graphite. But it was the Frenchman, Conte, who developed a method of mixing graphite and clay, baking it in a kiln, and then pressing it into grooves in wood; the resulting pencils could be graded in terms of hardness — the forerunner of the pencil as we know it today.

The two main types of coloured pencil in general use are those with soft, thick leads and those with thin, non-crumbling leads. The first variety are both waterproof and lightproof and come in the widest range of colours, while the latter have a more restricted colour range but are also waterproof.
There are also pencils with watersoluble leads that, when moistened, can produce an effect similar to watercolour.

Coloured pencil drawing by George Underwood for Cherry 'B'.

DUNKERQUE TOURIST BOARD/THE CLIENT BRIEF

THE CLIENT DUNKERQUE TOURIST BOARD
THE BRIEF TO PRODUCE A BROCHURE AND ADS TO PROMOTE DUNKERQUE AS A PLACE TO VISIT AND SHOP
THE AGENCY DAVIDSON PEARCE
ART DIRECTOR PAUL LYNCH
COPYWRITER TREVOR DE SILVA
ARTIST MICHAEL BISHOP

When people travel from Britain to the Continent through Dunkerque, they seldom stop, and therefore don't spend money. The client, the Dunkerque Tourist Board, wanted a promotion that would encourage people to take 'autumn-breaks' – for a week-end or longer. There were two problems about Dunkerque's image: it was not known as a tourist destination, but rather as the port from which the British were evacuated in the early stages of the Second World War; and the popularity of the other channel ports such as Calais and Boulogne, which are closer to England, making it more difficult for Dunkerque to attract short-term visitors.

The main copyline is 'A day is not enough' and the ads and brochure seek to show that the town is more than just a ferry port – it has very real attractions to offer the visitor. The free pencil style used was chosen because it can convey a romantic and attractive image for the town.

Interview with Paul Lynch and Trevor de Silva

DICK WARD What was your brief?
PAUL LYNCH The client wanted to attract visitors who would spend longer than a day in Dunkerque – they already had a small share of the day-tripper

ABOVE *The art director's rough for the 'fishing' ad.*

RIGHT *The finished press ad with the 'fishing' drawing.*

DUNKERQUE TOURIST BOARD /THE CLIENT BRIEF

There's more to Dunkerque than bringing back 2 boxes of Camembert.

Trying to discover Dunkerque in a day is rather like trying to do justice to the Louvre in half an hour.

For instance, it is quite easy to while away an entire afternoon exploring the bustling open-air market, supermarchés and specialist shops in the busy town centre.

Lunch in a bistro or dinner in a restaurant is equally likely to devour the hours, especially if you choose to sample the local speciality – a platter of fresh seafood.

Should you decide to discover the town's fine old buildings, like the Town Hall or the Leughenaer Tower – last remaining of the original 28 that once fortified the city – then you'd be well advised to set aside a whole day.

Such attractions make Dunkerque the perfect place to take a short break. And should you be left with a little time on your hands, then a spot of Christmas shopping in one of the three hypermarkets is definitely 'de rigeur.'

A DAY IS NOT ENOUGH.

Please send me details of Autumn/Winter breaks in Dunkerque, crossing from Ramsgate, on Sally Line.

Name_____
Address_____
_____ Postcode_____

Send the completed coupon to: Dunkerque Short Breaks, 17 Thame Park Road, Thame, Oxon OX9 3PG. Alternatively, see your travel agent.

DUNKERQUE FRANCE

DUNKERQUE TOURIST BOARD/THE CLIENT BRIEF

market, but the port wasn't known at all as a resort.
DW Is it a low-budget campaign?
TREVOR DE SILVA Yes. There wasn't a great deal of money available.
DW What was the timing?
PL We spent about a week on the presentation to the client.
TD We produced about four concepts in all, which were then
tested, so that took about another week.
PL There was a lot of deliberation before the Dunkerque Tourist Board decided to accept this agency.
TD We finally heard that we'd won the campaign about five weeks after we had produced the first concepts.
DW Did you do your own roughs?
PL Yes, but we also showed the client some examples of Michael Bishop's work.
DW Was the advertising campaign worked out by your media department?
PL Yes. As we had a small budget we

RIGHT **Michael Bishop's working trace for the 'fishing' ad.**

FAR RIGHT **The final proof of the 'fishing' drawing. This is a first-class example of free-style pencil drawing.**

BELOW **The reference photograph on which Michael Bishop based the 'fishing' drawing.**

DUNKERQUE TOURIST BOARD/THE CLIENT BRIEF

couldn't go to whole pages in the national press. So we had smaller ads in weekly magazines such as *Radio Times* and *Reader's Digest*, and a follow-up brochure from a coupon.
DW What made you use this particular style of illustration?
TD Michael Bishop has a French style of drawing – it is loose, colourful and vibrant.
PL He'd also done some drawings of restaurant façades in the same style that looked really good.
DW Why did you choose a loose pencil style? Did you want to make Dunkerque seem romantic?
PL Yes. And we had to emphasize that it is in France – a lot of people don't know exactly where it is and think it's in Belgium or Holland. So we included the French Tourist Board logo to make sure that nobody missed the location.
TD We also had to create a feeling of the place and get away from the war image. Dunkerque already has its fair share of the day-tripper market and we didn't want to lose that. But it is a long ferry journey, so people might as well stay longer.
DW Has the campaign been successful?
TD The first ads have had a good response – judging by the reply coupon.
DW How did you hear of Michael Bishop?
PL His agent had brought in his book some time ago and I always wanted to use him. This was the right job.
DW Did you give him a rough to work from?
PL We just gave him the work we had done for the presentation.
DW And the reference material?
PL We found the imagery, like the cyclists, by going over there.
TD We had to find some attractive scenes, and most of Dunkerque is modern, so it was a bit difficult to find the kind of imagery that people associate with France.
PL We had to find four or five scenes to give Michael Bishop a starting point, and they had to have some relationship to the area.

DUNKERQUE TOURIST BOARD/THE ARTIST

DW What about the copy?
TD It was important to see the town, to get the feel of it. The day we went it was pouring with rain, so it didn't look its most glamorous. But we had a good lunch!
TD The place has a lot more going for it than just duty-free shopping, and it is worth taking a few days to visit.
PL There are some great beaches as well!

Interview with Michael Bishop

DICK WARD How long did you have for each drawing?
MICHAEL BISHOP I did one about every two or three days and delivered them as I went.
DW What kind of pencils do you use?
MB I use soft, watersoluble coloured pencils.
DW How many pencils do you use on the black and white drawings?
MB A black and two greys – number 005 for the mid-tone, 003 for the light colour and the black is 009. Then I use a white for touching up, number 001.
DW Do you use a copyscanner (Camera Lucida)?
MB I don't use one very often and there is no need with this type of drawing, since the reference was quite vague. I had to combine images to arrive at an acceptable composition, and as it's in such a free style, it's a case of making a drawing that works.
DW Do you prefer an open brief or do you like a tight rough to work from?
MB An open brief. It gives me more scope and it's more interesting. In this case the reference wasn't very good so there was a fair amount of licence involved. The fishing is based on two reference shots and I've added the figure.
DW How did you do the drawings?
MB I cross-hatched part of the fishing drawing, but it's almost subconscious. I don't actually think 'I'm now going to do some cross-hatching.' If the lines all go the same way along the line of the bank it looks wrong, so I go over it to give it more form.
DW How do you lighten – with pencil or white gouache?
MB It's possible to lighten it slightly with a putty rubber (kneaded eraser) and if a more extensive amount has to be removed a hard rubber will do it. Or I might use a white pencil or a little gouache just to put in small strong highlights.
DW What paper do you work on?
MB Waterford smooth – in fact, it's a watercolour paper.
DW Do you mount it?
MB No. I draw straight on to it. I don't even bother to tape it down.
DW Do you start in any particular place on a drawing?
MB On this one I began with the figure – it's the most interesting and difficult part – and if it went wrong I'd start again. Once that was done I just worked my way around.
DW Do you start with the mid-tones?
MB Generally I put in the mid-tones first,

DUNKERQUE TOURIST BOARD/THE ARTIST

10 The final drawing

first, then come back when most of the drawing is finished and strengthen them with black and white.
DW Did you learn your technique at art college?
MB No, I wasn't taught to draw at art school – well, they were strong on life drawing but never tried to teach technique. So I set out to find the quickest way to get an image down on paper without getting bogged down with complicated equipment like a copyscanner (Camera Lucida).

1 Michael Bishop begins on the central figures using a black pencil.
2 He then starts the background using a grey pencil.
3 Using a mixture of pencils he establishes the background.
4 He uses a grey as he starts working into the sky.
5 Moving down the right-hand side of the drawing, he draws in the trees on the bank of the river.
6 Taking up a black again, he strengthens the trees.

7 Here he is strengthening the base of the trees and the far river bank.
8 Michael Bishop draws in the foreground and then starts on the detail. Throughout Michael Bishop uses a sheet of paper to protect each drawing from smudges as he works.
9 Moving back up to the sky, Michael Bishop strengthens it up a little more. Here he is using a homemade pencil extender – a small piece of rubber tube joining two pencils together – which means he can use short ends.

DUNKERQUE TOURIST BOARD/THE CAMPAIGN

ABOVE **The finished drawing of the ship which was used on the back of the brochure.**

LEFT **The artist's working trace for the 'windmill' ad.**

BELOW **The drawings inside the brochure suggest the kind of entertainment a visitor may enjoy.**

DUNKERQUE TOURIST BOARD/THE CAMPAIGN

There's more to Dunkerque than nipping over the Channel for lunch.

Trying to discover Dunkerque in a day is rather like trying to do justice to four courses of French cuisine in half an hour.

By way of example, a brief trip to the countryside will last for hours, as you'll find it almost impossible to pass through a beautiful little Flanders village without stopping to soak up the atmosphere in a quiet café or bar.

By the same token, trying to see the charming shops and boutiques in a single day is equally impossible. And the bustling open air market demands at least a morning.

A spot of sightseeing will become a cultural tour de force, as you take in The Belfry with its peal of 48 bells, and the museums of art – both fine and modern. Similarly, the surrounding towns have much to offer, Bergues with its impressive architecture and fortified Gravelines with its ancient ramparts and museum.

Possibly though, you'll fancy something a little more active, if so then the 10km of sandy beaches are more than perfect. Offering the ideal location for water sports, rambling and horse riding.

All in all, it makes Dunkerque the perfect place for a short break.

A DAY IS NOT ENOUGH.

ABOVE **The coloured version of the 'cyclist' ad. It shows how Michael Bishop's style is easily adaptable to colour.**

RIGHT **The finished ad featuring the windmill – a strong press ad with an interesting headline.**

TOP RIGHT AND BELOW **The artist's sketch traces for two of the small coloured drawings in the brochure.**

There's more to Dunkerque than whizzing round the hypermarket.

Trying to see Dunkerque in a day is rather like trying to read War and Peace in a couple of hours.

For example, a quick browse around the charming shops, boutiques and cafes is bound to end up lasting for hours.

A gentle stroll on the promenade will become a long ramble over the beautiful, sandy dunes.

A spot of sightseeing will turn into a cultural tour de force, as you take in The Belfry with its peal of 48 bells, and the museums of art – both fine and modern.

And if you don't happen to care for exploring windmills, you can always Christmas shop for bargains in either the hypermarkets or the busy supermarches and specialist shops in the town centre.

All in all, it makes Dunkerque the perfect place for a short break.

A DAY IS NOT ENOUGH.

Please send me details of Autumn/Winter breaks in Dunkerque, crossing from Ramsgate, on Sally Line.

Name
Address
Postcode
Send the completed coupon to: Dunkerque Short Breaks, 17 Thame Park Road, Thame, Oxon OX9 3PG. Alternatively, see your travel agent.

DUNKERQUE FRANCE

95

DUNKERQUE TOURIST BOARD/THE TECHNIQUES

The most common drawing tool of all is the pencil. Not only is it used as a drawing instrument in its own right, the pencil is an essential component in almost every other illustration medium. For his black and white drawings, Michael Bishop uses four pencils to produce the desired effect: two greys, a black and a white, but he could have achieved a similar effect with a graphite pencil. Pencil can create areas of tone as well as line, and can be used for flat areas as well as pattern and texture. Tone is generally created by building up lines or other marks – the denser and closer together these are, the darker the tone; for lighter tones the marks are finer and more widely spaced. Highlights are frequently represented by the lightness of the paper. Michael Bishop uses two kinds of rubber and a white pencil to create highlights, and occasionally might add white gouache to achieve a small hard light.

The type and quality of the line depends on how soft or hard the pencils are. The softer the pencil, the darker and broader the mark; the hard pencils create lighter and narrower lines. Very soft pencil drawings are vulnerable to smudging and should be sprayed with fixative (protective spray) on completion.

Although each artist develops a slightly different way of working, most of these individual methods are derived from a few basic ones – the most popular of which are stippling and hatching.

Choice of paper is also important when working with pencil, as the differing surface textures will influence the type of line and the density of tone produced. Michael Bishop prefers a smooth watercolour paper for his particular style.

Hatching
Parallel and graded hatched lines are frequently used to indicate form. Here the lines fade from dark to light.

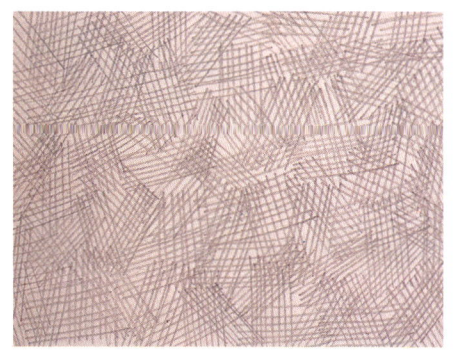

Hard-hatching
A hard pencil creates paler, narrower lines that are commonly used for hatching on technical subjects and for drawing lighter outlines.

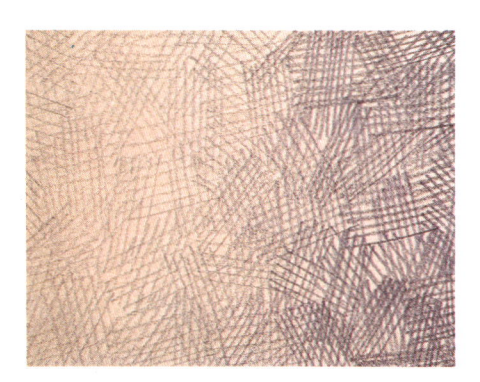

Cross-hatching
Another way of indicating form is to build up the surface with patches of cross-hatching, from dark to light.

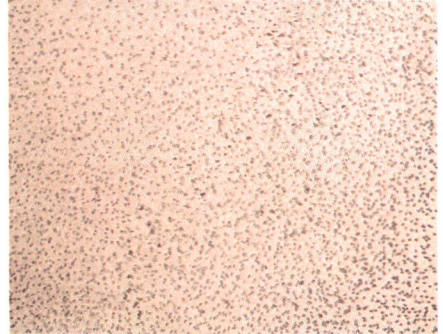

Stippling
Texture is built up with a series of dots. The denser stipple indicates the shaded areas.

Soft-Hatching
A soft pencil is used to produce characteristic broad dark lines, in this case a series of cross-hatched lines.

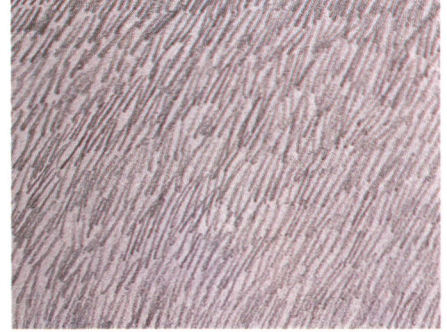

Flecks
Another method of building up shade and tone is to use short diagonal pencil strokes which are easy to control and fairly quick.

DUNKERQUE TOURIST BOARD/THE TECHNIQUES

Scribble
Loose but fairly evenly spaced scribbles are a useful way of shading or establishing tone.

Herringbone
Different patterns can be used to create tone and lend surface variety — such as this neat and regular herringbone texture.

RIGHT This very good free-style architectural drawing of Dunkerque's town hall was not used.

KLEENEX/THE CLIENT BRIEF

THE CLIENT	KLEENEX
THE BRIEF	TO CREATE TWO POSTERS, SIMILAR IN STYLE AND CONTENT TO A TELEVISION COMMERCIAL
THE AGENCY	DMB&B
ART DIRECTOR	JO HODGES
COPYWRITER	RUTH SHABI
ARTIST	AMY BURCH

Commissioned as part of a larger campaign based around a television commercial, two posters for Kleenex toilet tissue needed to be closely identifiable with the television advertising. The commercial is live-action and features two children, while the posters depict the children in tight coloured-pencil drawings. The illustrative technique used gives a velvet-like effect, which reinforces the very point the campaign is making about the product – its softness. The drawings are delightfully executed and are appropriate for a product of this nature, evoking a happy family life with contented children.

If photography had been used, it would have necessitated the same models who were used for the commercial, whereas with illustration the imagery merely has to remind the public of the television ad, thereby recalling the product automatically.

Interview with Jo Hodges

DICK WARD What was your brief?
JO HODGES The client wanted some posters to remind people of the television ad. As the commercial had some children in it, it made sense to keep to a simple format with a strong image of a child.
DW How many posters?
JH Just two – the little boy and the girl.

Kleenex Velvet.
The softest toilet tissue you can buy.

Softness is our strength.

The finished ad of the little girl captures the atmosphere of domesticity ideal for the product.

KLEENEX/THE CLIENT BRIEF

Kleenex Velvet.
The softest toilet tissue you can buy.

Softness is our strength.

LEFT *The finished ad of the little boy.*

BELOW *The art director's roughs for both ads — Jo Hodges relied on conveying a feeling to the artist rather than an accurate visual.*

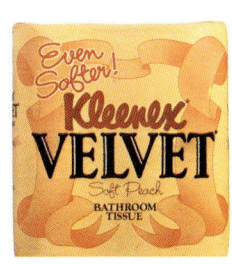

99

KLEENEX/THE REFERENCE

Some stills taken by the artist directly from the television to remind her of the atmosphere the client wants to achieve.

DW What was your timing?
JH Not very long, I think Amy had a week for each.
DW Why did you choose this particular style.
JH I'd seen Amy's drawings before – she had worked for somebody else in the agency. Her style was what I had in mind and I liked her drawing ability. But it took a long time to track her down.
DW Do you normally spend that much time finding an artist?
JH If necessary. This is an important client and you must make the right choice – it is essential to get someone who is reliable.
DW Did you consider a loose watercolour style?
JH I didn't think in terms of watercolour or charcoal or anything like that. I think this drawing style is the best to indicate softness and still link with the commercial.
DW Do you think you have more control with illustration or photography?
JH There is more control with photography. Illustration is often a gamble.

DW Is there currently a lot of interest in the more adventurous styles of illustration that are emerging?
JH I find all the different styles very exciting, although some of them are rather bogus with a few people just riding the band wagon.
DW Do you think of illustration as a photographic substitute?
JH No. I prefer to use it as a medium in itself – as a tool to convey a particular meaning.
DW Is the campaign designed to sell a specific product or to sell Kleenex as a corporate name?

KLEENEX/THE REFERENCE

JH To sell Kleenex as a whole but because it is television-led, it is aimed at the specific product.
DW Did you brief the agent or the artist?
JH I spoke to the agent, and briefed the artist on the telephone then sent the reference material to her. Not the normal way to brief an artist but she lives quite a long way away and we had to save time.
DW Did she do a rough?
JH Yes, she did a very good black and white drawing on tracing paper, and although it would have been too late to change my mind, it convinced me I'd made the right choice.

Interview with Amy Burch

DICK WARD What was your brief?
AMY BURCH To produce some appealing drawings of children, a boy and a girl.
DW Did the agency supply a rough?
AB Yes, but just very simple line sketches – nothing to go on really.
DW How long did each drawing take?
AB About five days for each.
DW Did you use a copyscanner (Camera Lucida)?
AB Yes I did. I don't always use it but on this job it made life a lot easier.
DW Do you take photographs for reference?
AB Yes, but I don't always work straight from a photograph. I often work from the actual object for still-life drawings.
DW What about figures?
AB Normally it's impractical to draw from life with commercial figure work – apart from the difficulty of getting models to stand still for long enough, it simply takes too long to find the right ones. So a photograph is far more convenient.
DW Do you improvise at all, or do you follow the photograph closely?
AB This particular job is fairly close to

Amy Burch's reference shot for the drawing of the little girl.

KLEENEX/THE ARTIST

the photograph – but I'm quite happy to improvize if necessary.
DW Do you use any particular technique?
AB No, I work instinctively. I didn't have any illustration training.
DW You didn't go to art school?
AB I did, but on a fine art course, which is a bit different from commercial work.
DW What kind of paper do you use?
AB Just ordinary cartridge (drawing) paper.
DW Do you mount or stretch it?
AB No, I usually work straight on the pad.
DW Do you ever have to scrap a drawing halfway through because it's gone wrong?
AB No, not normally. I don't have any problems in that direction; I tend to work quite slowly and carefully, and if I know what I'm doing I feel confident.
DW So you prefer a tight brief?
AB Yes I do. Although I'm much more confident now than when I first started, and can interpret a loose brief, but it's rare to be given one.
DW Why do you work in pencil?
AB It was almost by accident! I did some black and white pencil drawings at first, as they were the only materials I had to hand at the time. An illustrator friend showed them to his agent – they liked the drawings and took me on. I started to get work almost immediately and didn't have time to experiment with any other medium!

RIGHT *Amy Burch's first trace of the little girl, made with the aid of a copyscanner (Camera Lucida).*
FAR RIGHT *Amy Burch's rough, supplied to the art director after a telephone briefing.*

KLEENEX/THE ARTIST

Coloured pencils produce a distinctive effect that can be both delicate and precise. They are often used in mixed media work too, particularly with ink, watercolour and gouache, to lend contrasting lines and textures to flat colour and areas of wash.

Although most artists work in an instinctive way, the conventional technique is for colour to be mixed in built-up layers. This is known as overlaying, and may be carried out with finely rendered parallel lines hatched lightly and laid close together to form a flattish area of pale colour, or with looser strokes to create a coarser effect. Subsequent colours are overlaid in similar thin layers. Colours produced in this way have a shimmering effect that flat colour frequently lacks. Red laid over yellow, for example, produces an orange in which the red and yellow are visible; the orange created in this way is more interesting and vibrant than one produced with a single orange pencil. This technique has the advantage of enabling the artist to grade colour – producing an orange that changes gradually from yellow to red over a particular area.

An alternative mixing technique is to blend the colours 'optically'. Here the principle used is very similar to that of colour printing, with each colour being kept separate, but merging in the viewer's eye when looked at as a whole – thus strokes or dots of yellow and red give the optical impression of orange. If you look at the illustration of the little girl carefully you can see how the flesh tones are created with more than one colour.

Optical mixing is more suited to coloured pencil work than overlaid colour because the result retains the character of the pencil strokes, allowing the artist more freedom to produce spontaneous and creative effects. The technique also overcomes one of the major limitations of coloured pencils, namely the difficulty of overlaying more than two or three colours. This

KLEENEX/PENCIL

happens because the waxy colour tends to build up on the paper, causing the surface to lose its 'tooth' and become too shiny to work on.

Coloured pencils are at their best when creating texture and subtle effects. They do not lend themselves easily to work involving sharp tonal contrasts because it is not easy to build up very dark tones – even black and the darkest colours in the range are pale compared with their painted counterparts. Amy Burch deals with this problem by working over her drawings with an ordinary graphite pencil, strengthening contrast and helping the drawing's reproductive qualities.

BELOW LEFT **The 'little girl' drawing at an early stage. Amy Burch uses watersoluble pencils very lightly at first.**

BELOW RIGHT **The little girl after Amy Burch has started using a graded colour technique. She applies water with a no 6 ('standard') sable brush.**

ABOVE **The artist has blended the blue. The final stage of the drawing involves hatching on other colours and using a normal HB pencil to strengthen contrast.**

KLEENEX/THE TECHNIQUES

Optical mixing with strokes

When mixing colours 'optically', the pencil marks can be applied in a variety of ways. The artist makes no attempt to blend or mix the strokes and, although the result is an earthy neutral tint, the flecks of red, yellow and blue are quite distinctive. The amount of each colour can be varied to alter the overall effect — for example, if the artist had reduced the number of red marks in the examples below, the overall colour would have been green.

3 The strokes are applied in parallel, diagonal flecks. The lightest colour is laid first, in this case a yellow.
4 Once the blue is added the result is neutral, although the flecks of red, yellow and blue can be seen.

Overlaying colour

1 Using red and yellow, the artist overlays the pencil in regular parallel strokes. The lightest colour, the yellow, is laid first. Then red is added to produce orange, the strokes being laid at right angles to the underlying yellow.
2 Finally, blue is laid diagonally across the red and yellow to create a more neutral colour.

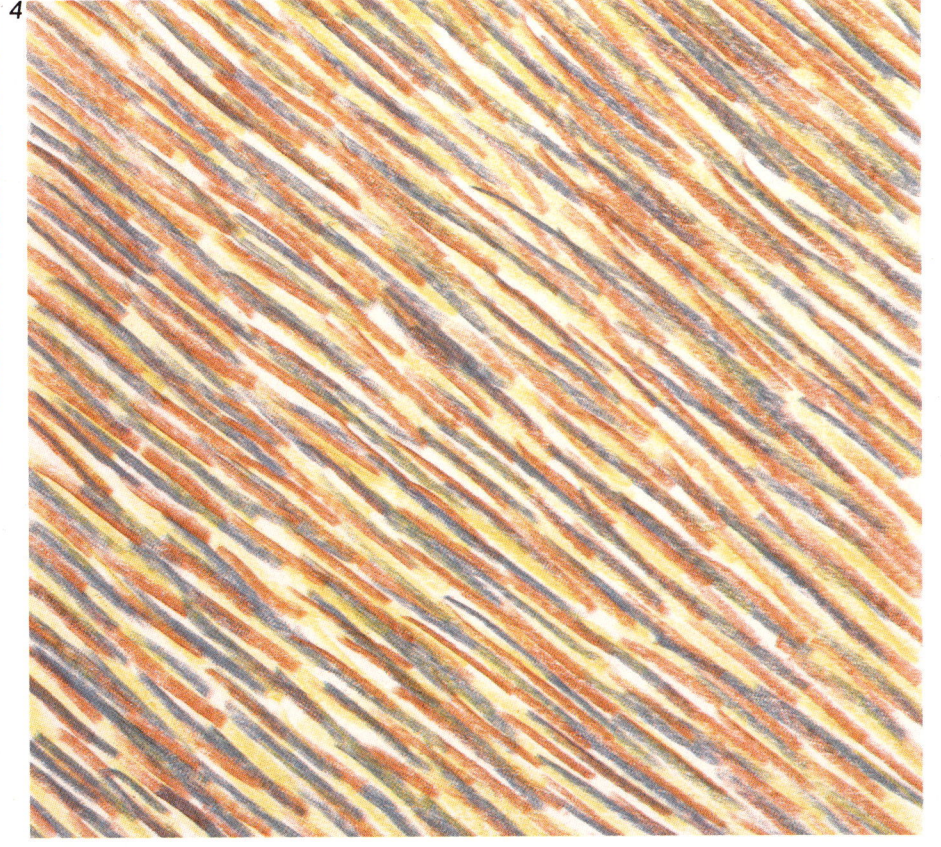

105

KLEENEX/PENCIL

Optical mixing with dots

This useful technique produces an even area of mixed colour, giving the artist maximum control with the overall colour. In this demonstration the artist uses colours densely, allowing very little of the white support to show through. However, the colour of the paper is frequently used in a positive way. Pastel shades and light tones can be created by spacing the coloured dots further apart and allowing flecks of white to show through. Using coloured or tinted papers can save time; red dots on a yellow background produce orange without the necessity of laying two colours.

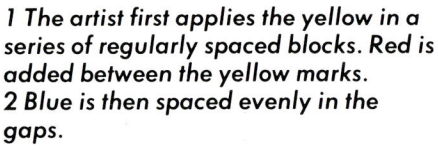

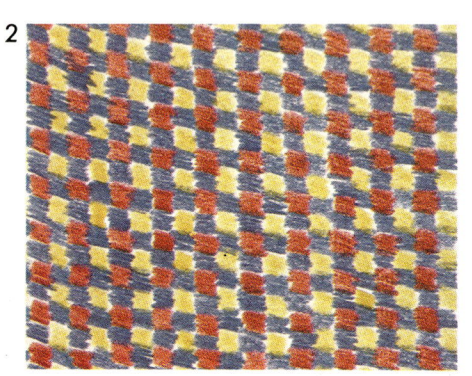

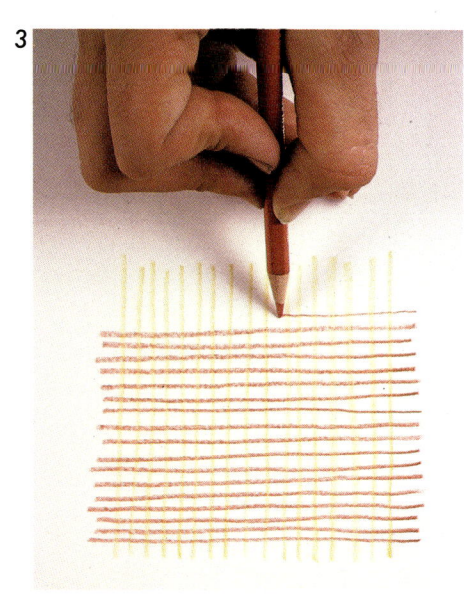

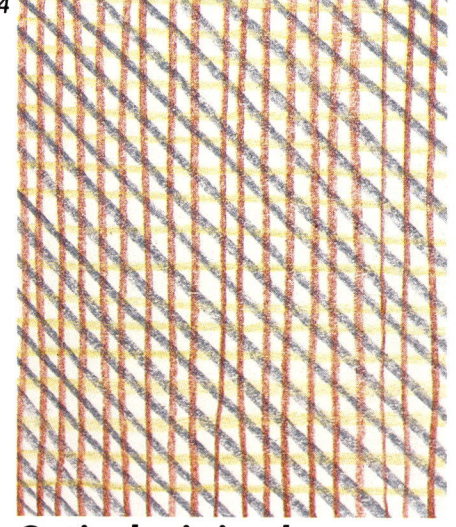

1 The artist first applies the yellow in a series of regularly spaced blocks. Red is added between the yellow marks.
2 Blue is then spaced evenly in the gaps.

Optical mixing by hatching

The principle here is the same as for the previous examples — the only difference is the method.
3 The yellow is applied first in evenly spaced parallel lines. The red is then cross-hatched over, keeping the spaces between the lines the same as the yellow.
4 Finally, blue is hatched diagonally across the yellow and red.

WATERSOLUBLE PENCIL

Used in exactly the same way as ordinary coloured pencils, the watersoluble pencil marks can be moistened to produce an effect similar to pure watercolour. Amy Burch uses watersoluble pencils to make what is effectively a normal coloured pencil drawing with a combination of the techniques previously described, and then uses water to dissolve and soften certain selected areas. Areas to be softened in this way should be drawn lightly at first, because heavy pencil strokes are difficult to dissolve and can show through a painted area. Large expanses of dissolved colour and flat washes are difficult to achieve and should be avoided.

The medium does require a little practice. Some colours go considerably darker when water is added, making the tones difficult to control. It is a good idea to test colours on a separate sheet of paper first, especially when wetting mixed or blended colours because some pigments are stronger than others and one colour is likely to dominate when wet.

Choice of support is important when using watersoluble pencils. Good quality watercolour or, as Amy Burch prefers, a heavyweight cartridge (drawing) paper is best. Whatever paper is used, make sure it is heavy enough to withstand water, otherwise the wet areas will buckle.

KLEENEX/THE TECHNIQUES

Graded colour

The density of the dissolved colour depends on the strength of the actual pencil marks. A drawn area of graded colour will retain its gradation even after being dampened, providing the water is applied sparingly and the colour doesn't run.

Blended colour

Colours can be blended together using water to avoid a harsh, noticeable join. The artist must first merge the pencil colours as much as possible, as although a hard edge between two pencilled colours can be blended it is difficult to achieve a smooth effect.

2 Clean water and a soft brush are needed to ensure a smooth transition from one colour to the next.

Mixed colour

It is possible to achieve a watercolour effect by using a small quantity of water on a soft brush; the pencil strokes must be light and even.
3 The artist dissolves areas of overlaid pencil to produce a watercolour effect.

Working wet

An alternative technique for using watersoluble pencils is to wet the paper first and then apply the coloured pencil to the dampened areas.
1 The artist starts by dampening the paper with a soft watercolour brush. The degree of dampness dictates the final effect.
2 The pencil is drawn into the dampened area and the colour starts to spread on contact with the water, flooding on to the damp paper. A partially damp support produces soft, feathery lines that are easier to control.
3 Further pencil drawing creates denser, brighter colour. If the paper dries before a particular colour is finished, more water can be added by loading the brush and allowing the water to flood across the damp area.

107

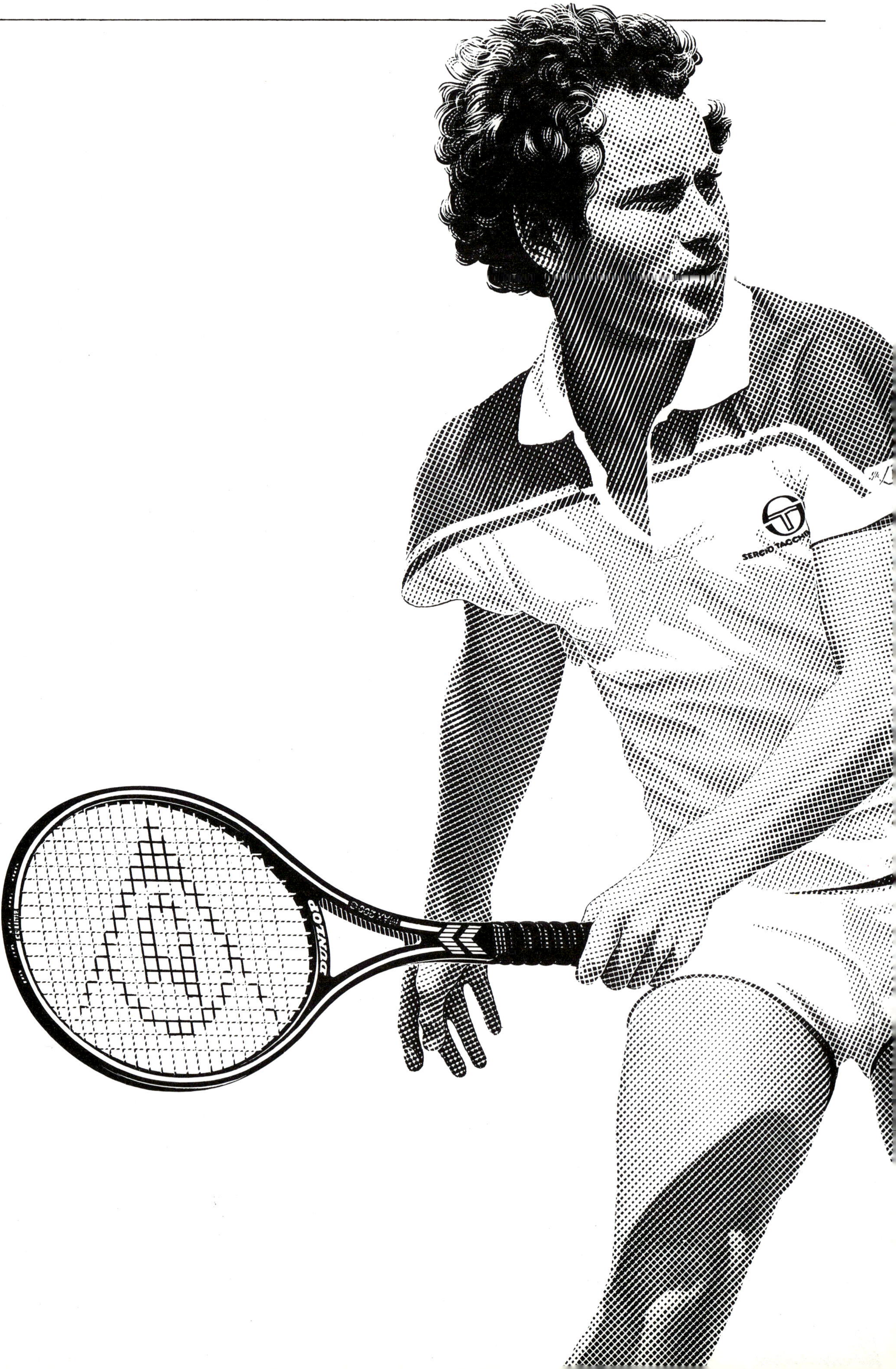

SCRAPERBOARD (SCRATCHBOARD)

The art of scraperboard is closely related to wood engraving and the techniques are similar. The only difference is the materials — instead of engraving on a block of wood, the artist uses a prepared board — either in white or black — the surface of which will be cut or 'scratched' away to create tonal effects in line. Styles vary from the mechanical and technical to looser, more spontaneous methods. Although scraperboard was at its peak, in terms of commercial use, in the 1950s and early 1960s, the craft is enjoying something of a revival as art directors discover its excellent reproductive qualities.

Scraperboard drawing by Tony Gilliam for Dunlop.

WARD WHITE/THE CLIENT BRIEF

THE CLIENT WARD WHITE
THE BRIEF TO ENHANCE THE IMAGE OF THE INTERNATIONAL RETAIL COMPANY WARD WHITE AND ATTRACT POTENTIAL INVESTORS
THE AGENCY YELLOWHAMMER
ART DIRECTOR JEREMY PEMBERTON
COPYWRITER ALAN PAGE
ARTIST PETER BLANDEMER

The artist in this campaign stumbled upon a 'new' style of scraperboard (scratchboard) that has rarely been used in advertising and which departs from the traditional, mechanical approach of the medium. Peter Blandemer actually draws with the scraper tool, and the end result is a spontaneous and strong image. The effect is a cross between a linocut and an etching.

The series of powerful and unusual ads stands out well in the newspapers, given the problems associated with the reproduction quality of newsprint. Generally scraperboard is an effective technique to use in newspaper advertising because the image is pure black and white, although the end result depends on whether the paper is under- or over-inked – in the first instance the blacks become grey and in the second, any fine white lines will fill in.

The images designed by art director Jeremy Pemberton are strong and simple and an intelligent answer to the exacting problem of corporate advertising where there is no product as such, but the client company seeks to establish its name in the mind of the reader and further enhance its reputation.

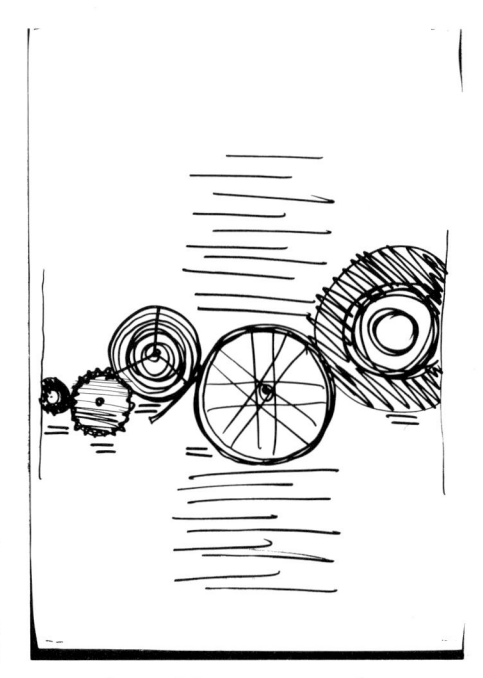

Interview with Jeremy Pemberton

DICK WARD What was the thinking behind these ads?
JEREMY PEMBERTON The wheels represent aspects of the Ward White business – they sell car spares, bicycles, hose pipes and circular saws, together with roller skates. The image makes the point that the company is moving – growing – and also shows its diversity.
DW Why did you decide to use illustration for this campaign?
JP Scraperboard illustration reproduces well in newspapers and has far more impact than photography. And we wanted a style that is typographical and precise. So we chose something with a lot of graphic impact. Initially we tried more traditional scraper drawings, but even though they were aesthetically pleasing, they weren't really strong enough – it looked as if they didn't have enough ink on them. This looser style really does stand out and it also means that we can use more interesting and slightly less obvious images.
DW What was your original brief?
JP To produce a series of corporate ads aimed at the financial sector, in order to attract potential investors in the company. We are looking at the small investor as well as the larger institutions such as pension funds and unit trusts.
DW What is your strategy?
JP We are advertising the client's management skills – how the turnover and profits have gone up every time a new business has been acquired. So when we wanted to show how the company has grown and diversified, we used a wheel. But we didn't want to limit it to a specific type of wheel with a certain number of spokes or a particular kind of bearing – we needed to be graphically vague and this is a wonderful way of doing it.

ABOVE LEFT *The art director's first rough. Different wheels suggest the diversity of the company and its growth.*

ABOVE RIGHT *In the second rough, the idea is refined and type added.*

RIGHT *A high-quality proof of the finished advertisement. The wheels have been straightened to emphasize the growth of the client's business.*

THE WHEELS OF FORTUNE.

As our latest interim results demonstrate, we're still growing exceptionally fast.

Turnover is up 50% to £365m. Pre-tax profit is a record £20.1m. After tax profit has almost doubled to £13m. And earnings per share have shot up almost 2p to 7.69p.

But it isn't just the company that's made a fortune in the last few years.

Anyone who had the foresight to put just £1,000 into Ward White shares five years ago would now have an investment worth over £6,000.

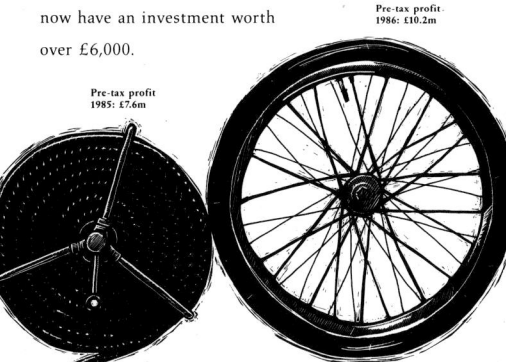

Pre-tax profit 1983: £2.2m
Pre-tax profit 1984: £3.2m
Pre-tax profit 1985: £7.6m
Pre-tax profit 1986: £10.2m
Pre-tax profit 1987: £20.1m

Proof, we believe, that our shareholders have been a great deal more fortunate than most.

Even in what has been called the longest and most profitable bull market of modern times, we have out-performed the market.

At Payless, Halfords and our most recent acquisition, Whitlock, the potential is only just beginning to be realised.

With highly skilled, in-depth Ward White management in place, we expect considerable organic growth from all these major retail groups.

And we are continually evaluating new, exciting opportunities for the Group.

All of which should lead our investors to one conclusion.

That our wheels of fortune still have a long way to go.

WARD WHITE
THE BUSINESS OF GROWTH

WARD WHITE/THE ARTIST

DW You are working within very narrow limits, aren't you?
JP Yes. We have to create full-page ads in black and white that will make people read what is essentially a dull piece of information. And because there are a lot of companies announcing their profits at the same time, we have to bring it to life and make it stand out.
DW How did you hear of the artist?
JP It was hard to find somebody with the right style. I was quite pleased with the first stage of the campaign but felt it would have been better with a looser and more dynamic illustration style to act as a foil to the delicacy of the type. We found Peter eventually after taking the usual route of contacting all the agents and looking through the illustration books.
DW Do you supply him with a rough?
JP Yes, I draw what is wanted in each case.
DW What was the timing on the job?
JP For the wheel illustration we had a couple of weeks, but generally there's not that much time. I would like to have 2 or 3 weeks always, but clients tend to spring things on us at the last moment, or the media department want to take advantage of favourable rates so we have to produce an ad very quickly and much faster than we would like.
DW How long did this ad run?
JP Generally, corporate campaigns run for about a month or so. This particular ad came out when the results were announced, and only ran for one day.
DW Do you feel you have more control with illustration?
JP You can commission illustration in various ways – on one hand, you can give artists very tight briefs and exact roughs – or you can give them loose briefs and no roughs, just tell them what the area and subject matter is and see what they come up with.
DW Are there many illustrators who can handle that?
JP If you're using very creative people you'd be a fool not to use them to their full abilities. I like this aspect of illustration – when I'm using someone creative, I'll give just a basic idea and

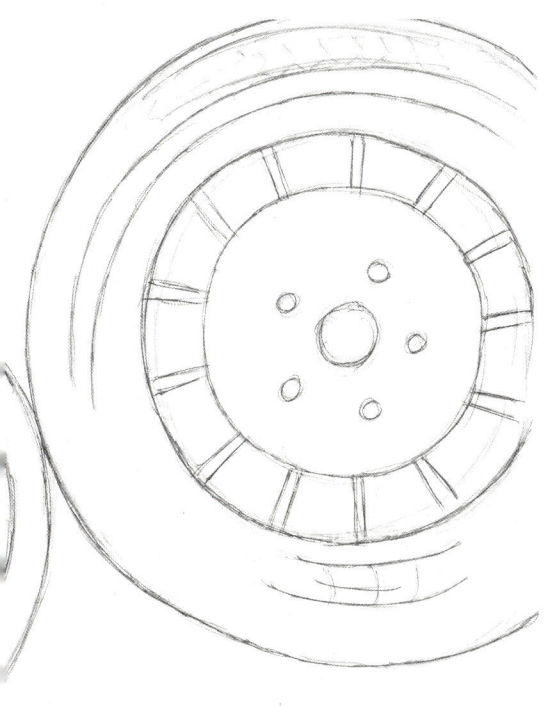

WARD WHITE/THE ARTIST

then it's very exciting to see what they've done when the job comes in. The other type of brief can be a problem because I'm lucky enough to draw sufficiently well to get an idea over to a client; then, if the illustrator doesn't stick very closely to the brief, the client may prefer the rough.

DW How would you contrast illustration with photography?

JP You tend to have much tighter control with photography, particularly if you're directing the shot yourself. You are there as the photographs are being taken, seeing the test polaroids, so you can change the lighting and the positioning. It is a much more controlled medium.

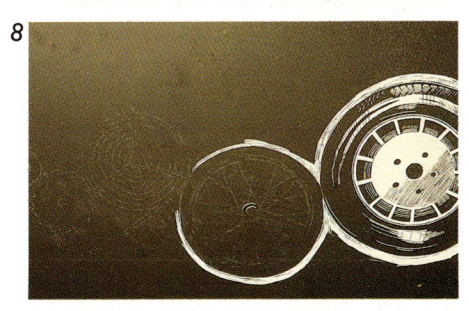

Interview with Peter Blandemer

DICK WARD How many ads have you done for Yellowhammer on the Ward White campaign?

PETER BLANDEMER Five.

DW Scraperboard (scratchboard) is normally very tight and mechanical. How did you develop your style?

PB I started doing a lot of pen and ink work when I was at college, but I wasn't really happy with it so I just played around copying things from library books and did some really awful pictures!

DW You taught yourself?

PB Yes, I've been working like this for about two years.

DW What's the first stage?

PB I might do a small drawing first to see how it looks, but if I've got a good rough, I'll go straight ahead into the drawing.

DW What do you use to trace down your image?

PB I use white pastel pencil, which shows up on the black. Most scraperboard artists use red tracing-down paper but it's difficult to get these days.

DW Do you simply rub the white pencil on the back of the tracing paper?

PB Yes. The way I work, I don't need an accurate trace anyway.

DW Do you use the ready-made scraperboard or do you paint it?

PB I use the ready-made black, which is unusual for professional artists, but it suits me.

LEFT *The artist's working trace. Peter Blandemer uses white pastel pencil on ready-made scraperboard (scratchboard).*

WARD WHITE/THE ARTIST

DW What scraper tools do you use?
PB A standard point, which can make a thin or thick line, depending on the angle.
DW You don't do a tight trace, but you use a compass or a copyscanner (Camera Lucida)?
PB No, I only work freehand, I haven't even got access to a scanner. If the client wants something really accurate normally they don't come to me.
DW How much time did you have to do the wheels?
PB About four days.
DW Is that longer than usual?
PB Yes, but I like as much time as possible because it doesn't always work first time.
DW Have you ever done any scraper drawings in the traditional way?
PB No, I've developed a style that I'm happy with. I like the medium – it's so instant, and it's a very satisfying way to work.

114

WARD WHITE/THE TECHNIQUES

Peter Blandemer has stumbled on a style that he can claim as his own. It looks simple and, compared to the mechanical approach of traditional scraperboard (scratchboard), it is, but it depends on an ability to draw rapidly and confidently with the scraper tool. This series of drawings demonstrates the surprising flexibility of a medium that has a reputation for rigidity.

Scraperboard illustrations can look photographic, or they can be broader in style – like Peter Blandemer's. But, as modern photographic processes can produce a printed effect from photographs which looks similar to scraperboard, the looser, more illustrative effects – the 'woodcut' look – are in demand, because they cannot be reproduced mechanically.

Scraperboard is popular with art directors for newspaper and magazine advertising because of its fine reproductive qualities. It reproduces well because no halftones or quartertones are necessary – the artwork is divided into black and white and all the tonal ranges are indicated simply in terms of black and white, with no grades of grey in between. Thus tone and form is achieved mainly by variations of pattern, making it ideal for printed reproduction. And because the work is normally reduced when reproduced, the patterns appear on a smaller scale, adding to the clarity and intensity of the tone.

Two basic techniques – known as 'white to black' and 'black to white' – are the foundation of all scraperboard (scratchboard) work, which is usually done in hatched and cross-hatched lines.

The ready-made, black-coated scraperboard is rarely used commercially, although Peter Blandemer uses it.

Two other images by Peter Blandemer for the campaign.

115

WARD WHITE/SCRAPERBOARD (SCRATCHBOARD)

Scraperboard is brittle and breaks easily and should be glued on mounting board with rubber solution (rubber cement) before work begins. Professional scraperboard is white, giving the artist the choice of drawing with black ink (black to white), or inking in with black those areas which are required to be scraped in white (white to black). Both approaches are frequently used in the same image to depict tonal extremes – for instance, in depicting a cylinder which is black on one side and light on the other.

To work black to white, the dark areas are inked in first; the light areas are left white. The artist first blocks in an area with black ink, usually waterproof. The ink must be applied in very thin layers, otherwise it leaves an unworkable skin on the surface; it is applied with a sable brush, quickly in parallel strokes, without overpainting the same area unless absolutely necessary.

To achieve a regular, even effect when applying the hatching and cross-hatching, artists use a drafting machine – a ruler fixed horizontally to a digital mechanism which measures the distance between each line. This distance, along with thickness of line, is extremely important. The wider the spaces and coarser the lines, the greater the tonal contrast; the finer and closer the lines, the 'greyer' the appearance of the finished piece.

Most scraperboard work is done on a larger scale than the finished reproduced piece. A typical scale would be 25 lines to the inch (2.5 cm) which would reproduce at 40 lines to the inch. The size of the finished work and the method of reproduction will govern the coarseness of the hatched lines.

Planning and precision are required because it is impossible to make major corrections. Minor alterations can sometimes be made with ink or opaque white paint, but it is extremely difficult to match up lines or textures – especially on large areas of even tone.

Typically, a scraperboard (scratchboard) artist working in the

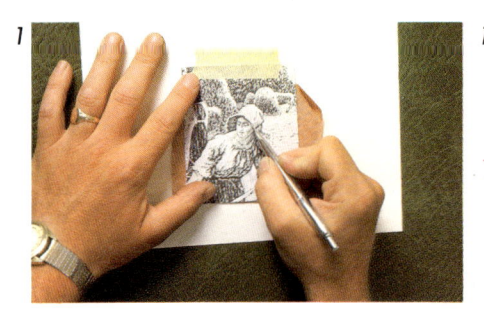

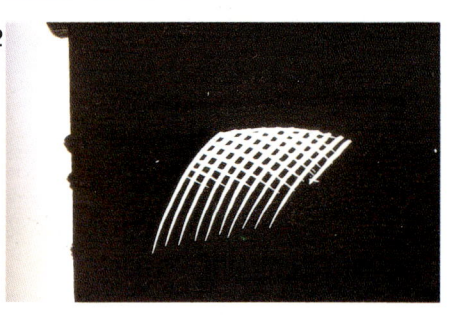

Tracing down an image
1 Tracing-down paper is normally used to transfer an image on to the scraperboard, although Peter Blandemer prefers to use pastel pencil. Start by placing the paper face down on the scraperboard and positioning the reference picture on top of this, taping in position if necessary. Use a hard pencil and trace firmly and accurately around the main outlines of the image.
2,3 The artist starts by outlining the figure with black ink and a fine sable brush. Then dark areas are blacked in.

Cross-hatching
1 Directional cross-hatching can be applied freehand to indicate surface form. This is how Peter Blandemer works, and is the basis from which all scraperboard drawings are built. The artist starts with a series of curved tapering lines.
2 This is then cross-hatched to produce a graded shading which can be adapted to suit any subject, ranging from irregular, natural forms to geometric constructions.

WARD WHITE/THE TECHNIQUES

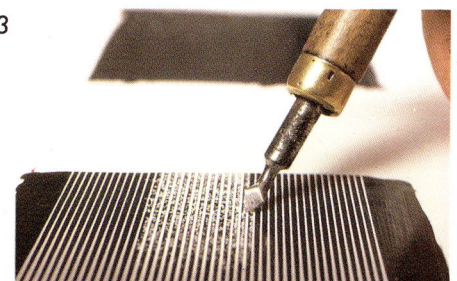

Tone and form

1 Here, simple cross-hatching is used to build up areas of tone and to describe form. The artist starts by blocking in the dark areas of the image, using a waterproof ink with a soft brush. It is important to keep the ink as thin as possible — a thick coat forms a skin that is difficult to work on.
2 When the ink is dry, an engraving point is used to hatch a series of regular parallel lines. The drawing instrument is attached to a drafting machine that regulates the line spacing.
3,4 Light and dark are depicted by varying the spaces between the lines and the thickness of the lines themselves — a method frequently adopted to suggest a rounded surface or to establish form in terms of light and shade. Here the artist is lightening an area by thickening selected lines across the hatched tonal plane.
5 Strong white cross-hatching increases the lightness of the worked area, reducing the original blacking-in to a series of regularly placed dots.
6 Conversely, the hatched area can be darkened by cross-hatching in black ink with a technical pen.
7 Further work can be done with an engraving point to create highlights.

117

WARD WHITE/SCRAPERBOARD (SCRATCHBOARD)

traditional method uses detailed photographic reference. The main lines of the photograph are usually precisely followed using tracedown paper. This contrasts with the way Peter Blandemer simply uses white pastel pencil rubbed on the back of his trace.

To depict certain textures such as woodgrain, leather, fur, hair and skin, most artists develop their own personal techniques. In the demonstrations on this page, for instance, the artist shows how to portray metal, woodgraining and skin, but many other approaches could also be devised. None of these techniques, however, is relevant if not seen in context: leather will not look like leather unless it is portrayed on a recognizable leather object.

The tools for working white to black can be brush, technical pen or dip pen. For scraping white lines on to black areas, specialist scraperboard tools are available. In some of these demonstrations, old engraving implements were used.

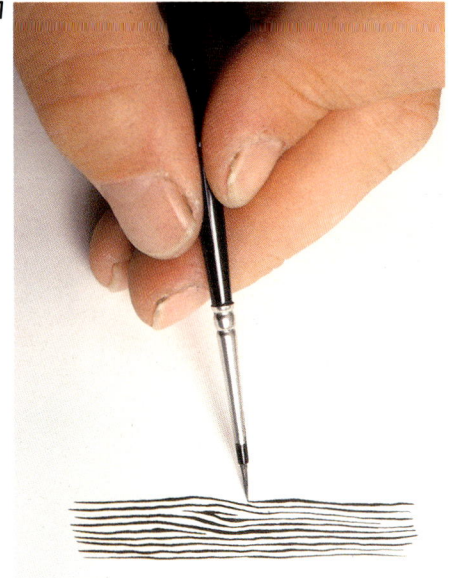

Woodgrain
1 Using a fine sable brush, the artist starts by copying the surface pattern of grained wood.
The lines are applied loosely, the artist painting with a free wrist movement to create a natural, undulating pattern.
2 Some of the painted lines are scored with a fine point to imitate the fibrous appearance of the grain.

Metal
The car wheel shown here, a detail from a larger work, shows the wide range of hatching and cross-hatching techniques employed to indicate the various textures and surfaces of the subject.
The regular hatching and cross-hatching on the body of the car and on the tyre was rendered with the help of a drafting machine; this mechanical texture is broken and scratched back in certain places to suggest metallic highlights. The ground was initially drawn with freehand strokes and then cross-hatched with fine parallel lines.

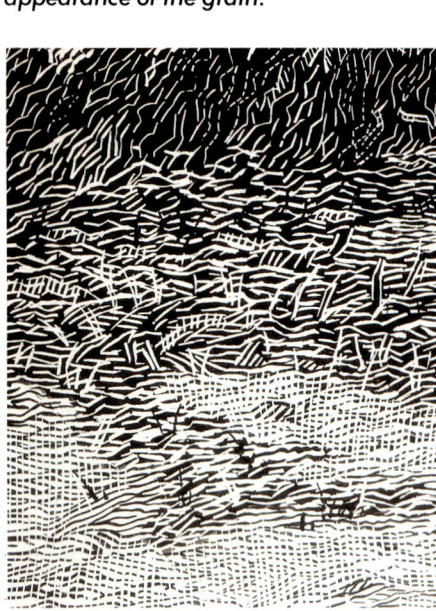

Sky and grass
1 A typical method of showing the nebulous forms of sky and cloud — common but difficult subjects — is with built-up areas of lightly toned freehand cross-hatching.
2 Short, confident marks describe an area of uneven grass — another difficult subject. The artist has aimed for a general impression rather than detail.

Skin

1 Mechanical hatching and cross-hatching is not restricted to hard-edged subjects. The techniques can be adapted to suit any image, and are generally used for a subtle and controlled effect rather than to suit a particular subject.

In this advertising illustration, the artist used exactly the same techniques for the soft skin of the woman's hand as for the rigid, geometric shapes of the computer in the background. Note the convincing illusion of tone.

2 The detail of the thumbnail and part of the thumb shows how the areas of lights and darks have been simplified and broken down into shapes of cross-hatched tone. The thumbnail is cross-hatched diagonally and the computer horizontally. The rounded forms of the thumb and finger are described with graded cross-hatching, with the hatched white lines thickened towards the illuminated edge.

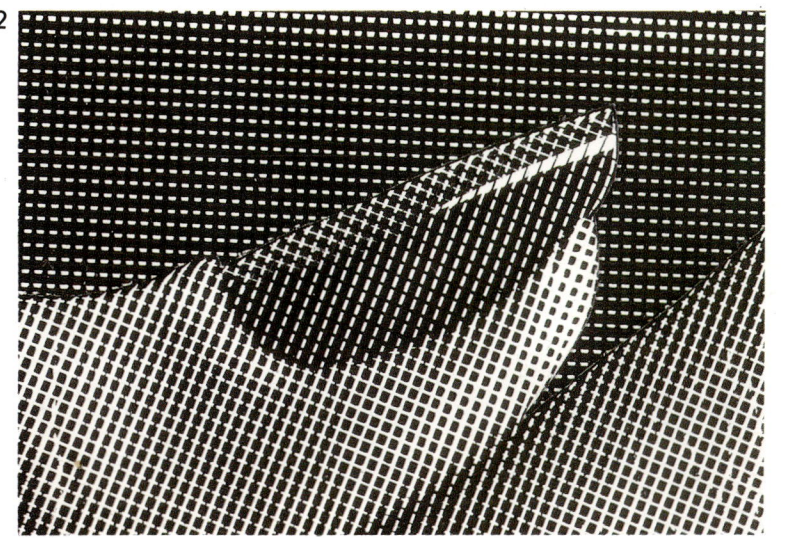

RUDDLES ARE GOING TO TOWN

Here's how we're putting County on the map: 1. With a £1.3 million National advertising spend, including full colour, in the Sunday supplements. 2. Ruddles County will be going places on bus sides too. 3. And we're well on the way to making a name for ourselves in the high street, on 48 sheet posters. 4. We'll soon be pouring all over Britain. 5. There are (County or Best Bitter); in a wide mouthed bottle be ready for Ruddles. It's going to be the most

CARTOON

The cartoonist's ability to draw instantly and without reference is one of the most enviable – and one of the rarest. The talent to create a scene, or a character, or atmosphere with the minimum of line is the essence of this art. A few strokes of the pen or pencil make a story which conveys a message through humour. The cartoon is a very powerful medium – witness the number of cartoonists who have been imprisoned over the centuries, and the effect of the cutting political cartoon. Cartoons are used in advertising to sell a multitude of products and cause a chuckle at the same time. Advertising should not antagonize the potential customer, and the old axiom of 'if in doubt, make 'em laugh' still holds true.

Cartoon by Ainslie Macleod for Ruddles Beers.

ANGOSTURA BITTERS/THE CLIENT BRIEF

THE CLIENT	ANGOSTURA BITTERS
THE BRIEF	TO CREATE A NEW MARKET FOR ANGOSTURA BITTERS, A WELL-KNOWN PRODUCT IN THE SOFT DRINKS SECTOR
THE AGENCY	TAVISTOCK
ART DIRECTOR	ROBIN NASH
ARTIST	LARRY

The Angostura bitters campaign is a very successful one. The agency has spent a limited budget very astutely to reach its target audience. The choice of cartoons is ideal for advertising on the underground (subway) because travellers are often uncomfortable and a little light relief is very welcome.

The problem of increasing sales for a product that is well known, but that has a narrow traditional use, is a perennial one – and the idea of creating a new soft drink is both sound and socially acceptable. A cartoonist such as Larry, with his wonderful brand of humour, makes the point simply, immediately and memorably.

The skill of the artist and the enthusiasm with which he tackles the brief shows in the following pages. Although Larry insists that his humour is typically English, few people could resist smiling at his images.

Interview with Robin Nash

DICK WARD What made you choose a cartoonist for this campaign?
ROBIN NASH We had a small budget and had to reach as many people as possible. Because we were advertising on underground cards, I thought that a cartoon would be different enough to gain attention – particularly since there's a captive audience and it's the right place to create a smile, yet cause impact at the same time. Most of the ads on the underground are very garish, so these black and white line drawings stand out well and spot colour helps to make them noticeable.
DW What was your brief?
RN The client's product is known throughout the world, but is really only associated with pink gin, so we had to create a new market for it – to make it an acceptable non-alcoholic drink in its own right.
DW There seems to be a market opportunity for the right soft drink because of the drinking and driving problem.
RN That's right. Our trade campaign was designed to promote a responsible attitude from landlords and bar staff – to try and encourage them to recommend our drink as an alternative to alcoholic drinks.

ANGOSTURA BITTERS/THE CLIENT BRIEF

DW Has the campaign been successful so far?
RN Yes, according to the retailers, people are asking for the drink in bars. We only have to get each pub or hotel to buy one or two more bottles of bitters a year and the sales will virtually double – because so little of it is sold. There is an existing market – nothing else makes a pink gin pink – but the problem is that it only takes one drop per glass. We're trying to make people realize that it's great to drink with tonic water.
DW Do you find that you have more control with illustration?
RN No, not really. Illustrators tend to do what's asked of them but in their own way. Photography is more controlled from the outset, as you can direct every

BELOW *The finished ad used as an underground (subway) card. Larry created this drawing from a headline supplied by the agency.*

TONIC! SUCH SOPHISTICATION! MEMBERSHIP WAS UNOPPOSED.

123

ANGOSTURA BITTERS/THE ROUGHS

aspect of it, and the photographer does it your way, so any problems should be seen there and then.
DW Did you give Larry copy lines and let him come up with the images, or did you give him roughs?
RN Both, in this case. Sometimes Larry told us which ones would work and which wouldn't.

Interview with Larry

DICK WARD How did your style evolve?
LARRY All cartoonists start off by copying somebody else at first, and then get fed up with that, and gradually their own style emerges. When I first started, I did a job for the magazine *Punch* – they hadn't seen my work before and somebody in their art department joined up all the lines!

But it's a mystery to me exactly how people arrive at their styles. Ronald Searle was a big influence and Giles spawned a lot of copyists. The big noses are about the only thing I've cribbed – from Bosk, the French cartoonist. In fact I draw the same type of person all the time, mostly based on working-class characters. I find it very difficult to draw a 'sophisticated' person.
DW What makes a good cartoonist?
L Being able to visualize things and to draw anything quickly without reference. You have to be obsessed with humour and then be able to draw – not the other way round. People have either got it or they haven't – if they have, you can see it immediately.
DW Did you go to art school?
L Yes, I did a lot of life drawing in my day, so I can draw figures in any position. I owe my loose line to my art master. I used to draw very stiff mechanical lines, and he showed me how to get a more sensitive line by altering the pressure on the pencil. I was like every student; I wouldn't sharpen my pencil and I put a heavy outline on things. He taught me to look at things properly – when you draw an arm, for example, the elbow needs emphasis, and the intermediate lines vary in thickness. This is what gives a drawing a bit of life. The wobbly line can give it a kind of animation and movement. All this is subconscious. You don't say to yourself I'll do this and I'll do that, it becomes completely automatic.
DW What do you think of art schools today?
L There's not the same emphasis on drawing. We had a year drawing from statues, and then went on to life drawing for another year. You decided what to specialize in after two years of learning to draw. I think the creativity is still there but they're not teaching technique. Learning technique gives you the tools, the creativity can follow. Knowledge of the basic drawing skills encourages creativity.
DW What was your brief on this job?
L The agency conceived the situations, gave me the captions and, in some cases, roughs as well. I prefer it, though, when the agency just wants gags, and has got an open mind – then they develop the campaign around the gags. Sometimes an agency thinks up the jokes and the client accepts them but then they won't work visually. In this campaign there were one or two that didn't really come off, where you couldn't see the bloke with the Angostura because he would have been lost in the crowd.
DW Why do you think this campaign works?
L The underground (subway) is a good place to advertise because cartoons work particularly well there. Cartoons are not used enough on posters (billboards) – which is a pity because that is where they can really work well. So many posters have too much copy and usually there isn't enough time to read it all.
DW What size do you work?
L I usually work small, on a standard sheet of typing paper, although here the format of these ads is slightly wider than that.
DW What materials do you use?

ABOVE **The agency rough to present to the client, using a photocopy of Larry's drawing and showing the position of the product photograph.**

RIGHT **One of the ads running concurrently with the 'punk'. The use of spot colour to highlight the product is a clever feature of this campaign.**

ANGOSTURA BITTERS/THE ROUGHS

RA AND YOU-KNOW-WHO! SUCH SOPHISTICATION!
WONDER HIS MEMBERSHIP WAS UNOPPOSED.

THANKS TO THE ANGOSTURA AND TONIC OUR DRIVER MISSED A NIGHT IN THE CELLS, A CRUSHING HANGOVER, A TRUCK, TWO CYCLISTS AND A NUDE ROLLER-SKATER.

ANGOSTURA BITTERS/THE ARTIST

L I use a mapping pen (steel crow quill) – most cartoonists do – with Indian ink. Some of the younger generation use a rapidograph (technical pen), but that gives a very rigid line. One of the problems I have is that by the time I get used to a pen and it's worked in, it breaks, because they only last about three weeks!

DW Do you do a pencil drawing first?

L No. You lose the spontaneity. Of course, it's trial and error – I'll scrap one and have another go at it. I do the first drawing and if it's not right I'll put it under the next sheet of paper – that's why I use ordinary typing paper – you can just see through it. Then I'll do it again using the first one as a guide, I don't trace it off as such. It never comes out the same anyway.

TOP *The art director's first rough for another ad in the same campaign. It was rejected as being too partisan.*

CENTRE *The art director's second rough on a tennis theme – discarded as obscure.*

BELOW *The final image for this ad. Note the simple way Larry portrays heat.*

ANGOSTURA BITTERS/THE ARTIST

DW You find typing paper better than normal layout paper?
L Yes, it's just robust enough to be handled. Layout paper is too thin; it's nice to draw on but just a bit too delicate – the solid blacks cockle up.

DW How long does it take you to finish a drawing?
L It depends on the content, anything from 10 minutes to half an hour.
DW Is most of your work editorial or advertising?
L I've never been a newspaper cartoonist. I tend to be useful to charities and organizations like life assurance companies where you need a bit of humour to sell the product!

Two other ads running concurrently with the 'punk'.

WITHOUT THE ANGOSTURA AND TONIC, THE SOLO SYNCRONISED SWIMMING EVENT WOULD HAVE BEEN LESS THAN RIVETING.

EXILED TO THE TRACKLESS WASTES OF THE OUTFIELD, NOTHING SUSTAINS THE WILL TO LIVE LIKE AN ANGOSTURA AND TONIC.

ANGOSTURA BITTERS/CARTOON

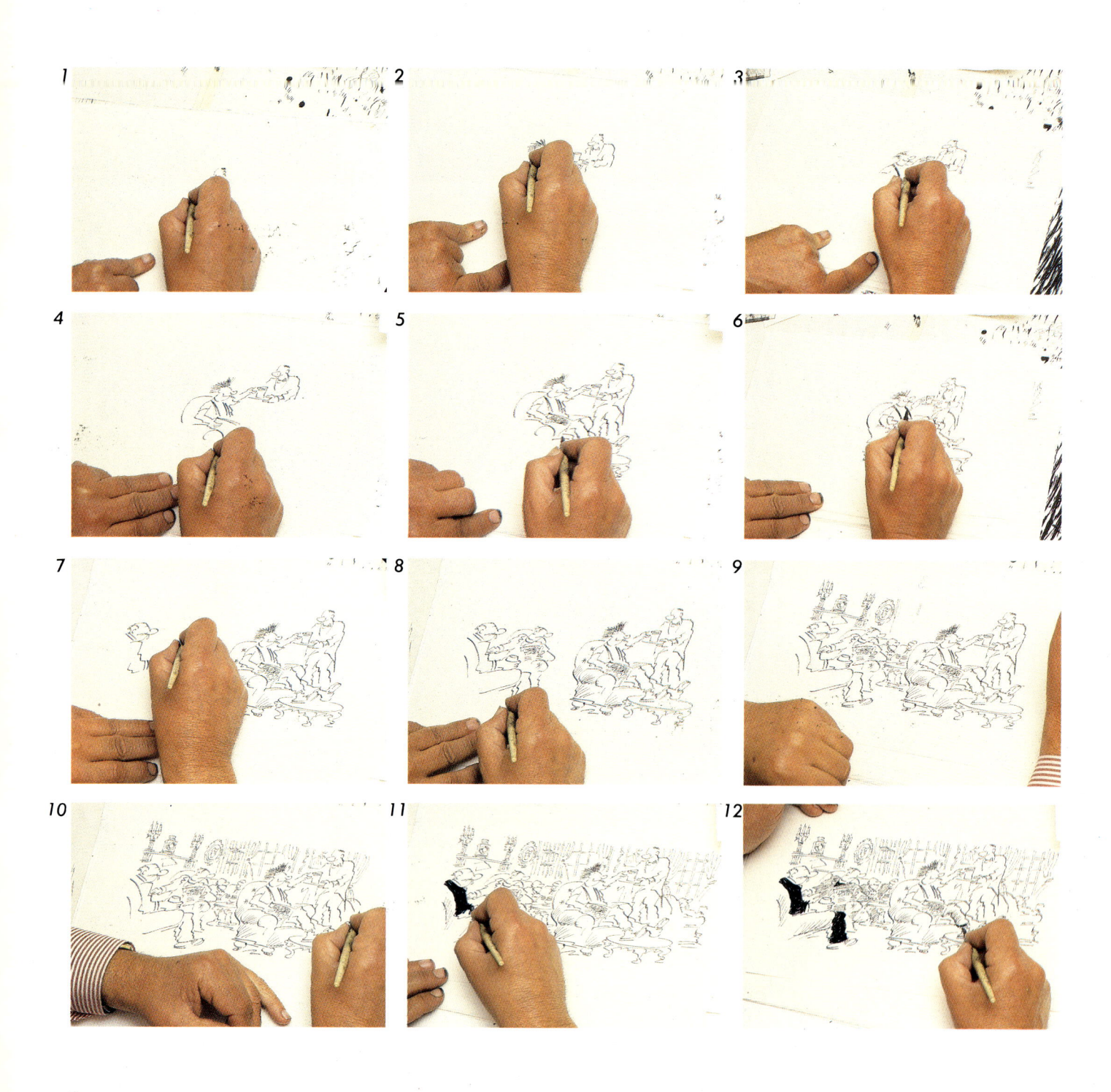

ANGOSTURA BITTERS/THE TECHNIQUES

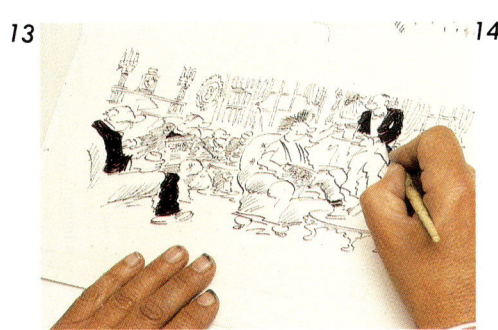

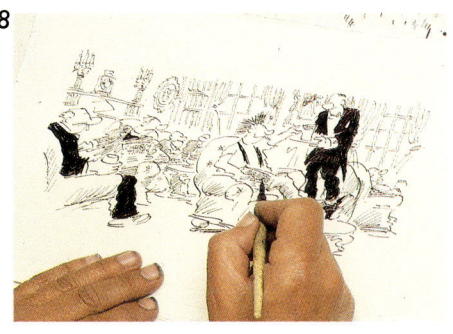

The following images show Larry recreating the 'punk' illustration. This drawing was finished in about 15 minutes without any pre-sketching or reference. This is an enviable talent that cannot be priced in hours worked. All cartoonists are unique and most work with this kind of speed and confidence. Larry's spontaneity and sense of humour show in his work.

The central character is drawn first to get the correct positioning, followed by the waiter – the rest just flows. In the original drawing, characters were put in on the left merely to fill the composition, but then became an important part of the whole illustration. The background is literally just a few lines, but somehow immediately suggests a gentlemen's club. The atmosphere of stunned amazement and affronted dignity is portrayed perfectly.

This cartoon demonstrates how an image can be achieved in the simplest possible way. The combination of Larry's gentle humour and draughtsmanship creates a situation that is instantly recognizable and successfully sells a traditional product.

ANGOSTURA AND TONIC! SUCH SOPHISTICATION! NO WONDER HIS MEMBERSHIP WAS UNOPPOSED.

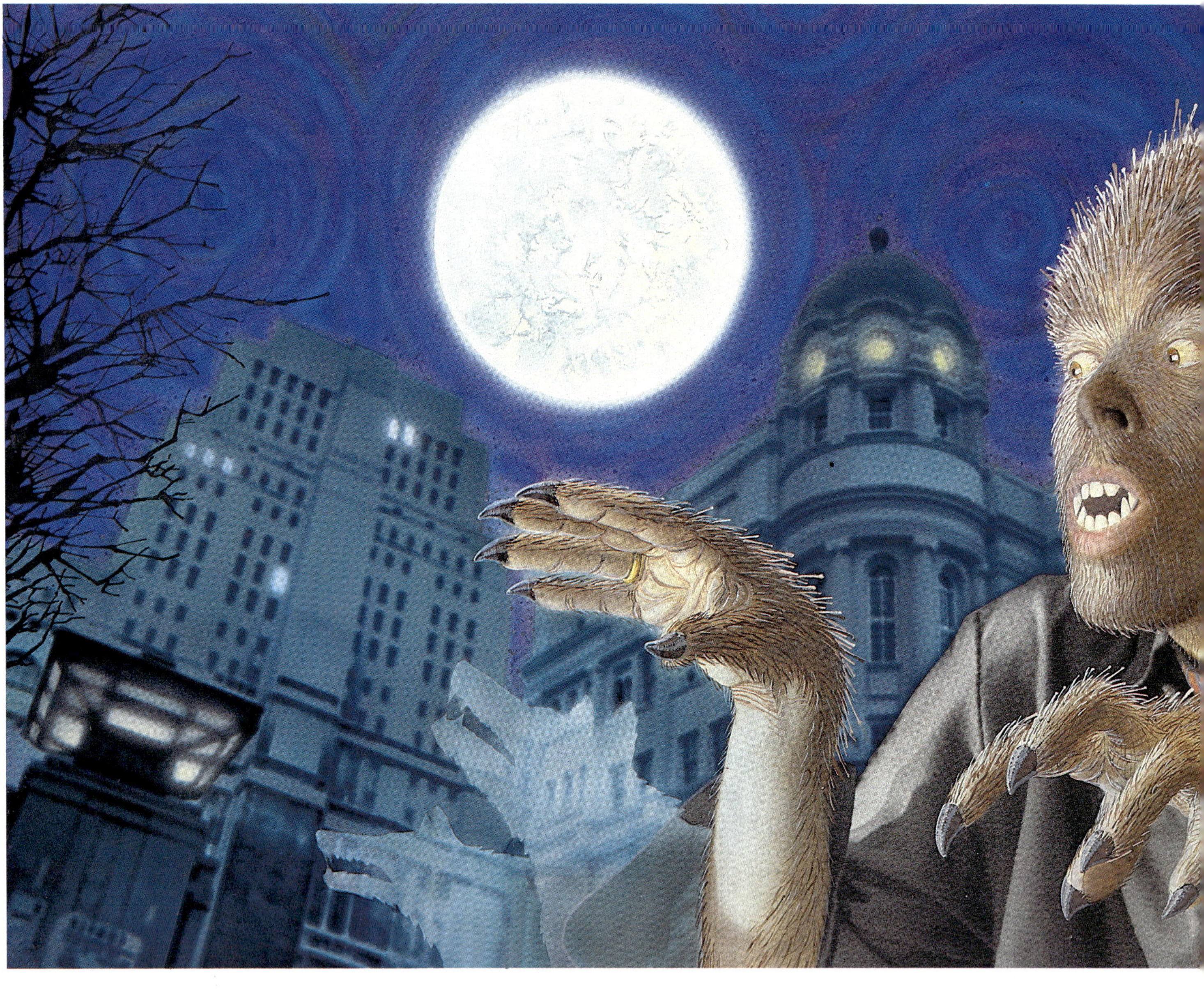

PHOTOMONTAGE

Photo-montage has been used as a technique by illustrators and artists ever since the camera was invented and plays a prominent part in the history of *avant-garde* and anti-establishment art.

The simplest photo-montage method involves cutting out sections of different prints and combining them to form a finished image. A more complicated method involves making up the image in the darkroom using negatives or colour transparencies.

The technique of superimposing unlikely and disturbing imagery was used to great effect by Man Ray and his fellow Dadaists in the 1920s and 1930s and later by the anti-Nazi artists, who included Raoul Hausmann, Hannah Hoch and John Heartfield. In fine-art collage, not only photographs but an amalgam of materials and objects are pasted together to create the final image; this is fairly rare in advertising, where usually photographs only are used.

Photo-montage illustration by Simon Fell for Commercial Union Insurance.

BRITISH RAIL/THE CLIENT BRIEF

THE CLIENT	BRITISH RAIL
THE BRIEF	TO SELL THE OFFER OF 80% DISCOUNT OFF YOUNG PERSON'S RAILCARD FOR ONE MONTH
THE AGENCY	SAATCHI AND SAATCHI
GROUP HEAD	ROB KITCHEN
ART DIRECTOR	LINDA CASH
COPYWRITER	LORNA MURRELL
ARTIST	GEOFF HALPIN

When a campaign is specifically targetted, as this was, it is a good opportunity to try something bold and adventurous.

The campaign started with a radio commercial that created a fifties science-fiction atmosphere, and then continued with a poster and magazine advertisements. The route chosen by the creative team for the radio commercial predetermined, to a certain extent, the style of the finished illustration. Geoff Halpin was the natural choice as artist, an illustrator/designer with a unique feel and knowledge of the period.

He captured the atmosphere of the radio commercial perfectly and the campaign successfully reached a specific market in a limited amount of time.

There are several ways this brief could have evolved. A very glossy airbrush style might have been appropriate or a painting that looked like the cover of a science-fiction paperback, for example.

Even a comic or strip-cartoon method might have been suitable. In the event, the method chosen brilliantly reflects the humour in the radio commercial, and the overall result is a cleverly co-ordinated campaign.

Although most of the 'young persons' of today have probably never heard a fifties science-fiction serial, both the radio commercial and the graphics are highly evocative and create a feeling of recognition in the mind of the consumer.

Linda Cash and Lorna Murrell are both relative newcomers to advertising. This was Murrell's first job after leaving copywriting college, and then being unemployed for 16 months. After art school, Cash spent 6 weeks gaining work experience at Doyle Dane Bernbach before joining Saatchis where she had had 18 months experience before the start of this campaign. Not the usual route for a creative team. This was their first campaign and, incidentally, a highly successful one, producing about

BRITISH RAIL/THE CLIENT BRIEF

20,000 more enquiries than usual to British Rail in that month. Credit is due to Saatchis for recognizing new talent and Rob Kitchen for encouraging it.

Geoff Halpin began his career in graphics, working in Zimbabwe and Zambia where the lack of such things as typefaces and Letraset resulted in him becoming a very original lettering designer, although in this case, hand-drawn lettering wasn't used. He became known for his fifties style almost by accident after doing a lot of record work in the late sixties and early seventies.

It is a winning combination – an adventurous client, imaginative creative team and a unique artist. This is a delightfully original piece of work.

Interview with Linda Cash and Lorna Murrell

DICK WARD Was your first brief from the client or the account handler?
LINDA CASH From the account handler. It was to get over the proposition that for one

FACING PAGE *The finished magazine ad is a very strong image.*
ABOVE AND LEFT *The first agency roughs by the art director and copywriter.*
ABOVE RIGHT *Some of the artist's reference material collected from old magazines.*

month there was an 80 per cent discount on Young Person's Saver Fares. The client wanted a strong and unusual image that would appeal to young people.
DW What made you decide to use Geoff Halpin and this particular style?
LORNA MURRELL We wrote the radio script first and that had a strong science-fiction flavour. So it made sense to retain the same feeling.
DW How did you hear about Geoff Halpin?
LC Through Rob Kitchen, our group head. He knew of Geoff's work and that he was interested in the fifties. He sounded ideal, and he was.
DW How did you go about making up the first rough?
LC By looking in old magazines. We bought some old copies of the *Saturday Evening Post* and things like that. That's where we found the sort of people and imagery we wanted to use. At first we were thinking of having objects scattered

BRITISH RAIL/THE ARTIST

around, flying, but it became too messy and Geoff agreed.

DW How long did it take from the brief to the finished art?

LC It was quite a rush. We were briefed on the radio commercial first, on the 9th December, and we presented that 3 days later. We briefed Geoff on the 29th and he produced the rough on the 2nd January. His finished artwork was ready on the 7th.

DW That's very fast all round, especially for the radio script. How did you arrive at the concept initially? Why did you think of doing it as science-fiction?

LM British Rail's offer was so good that we thought young people would be disappearing all over the place. They'd be 'vanishing'. The question was where had they gone and why?

DW Geoff told me his first choice of typeface was changed. What was the story on that?

LC He designed a very interesting typeface, but British Rail prefered to use their standard Futura. But I think the final ads worked really well. The client's very pleased and so are we.

Interview with Geoff Halpin

DICK WARD Where do you find all your references for this kind of job?

GEOFF HALPIN They come from lots of different sources, old magazines of course and lots of other different bits of pictures that are put together then changed.

DW Have you got a reference library or stock of material that you've built up over the years?

GH I have some material but I tend to find individual pieces for each job as it happens. Most of this came from the Vintage Magazine Shop. We got a big pile of fifties-imagery magazines, photos and so on – and went through picking out relevant bits and pieces.

DW Did you work hand in hand with the art director or did you present her with roughs?

GH We chose the actual material together and then I did a rough from that.

DW How do you start the artwork once you've got the rough approved?

SAATCHI & SAATCHI COMPTON LTD.
REGISTERED OFFICE: 80 CHARLOTTE STREET, LONDON W1A 1AQ TEL 01-636 5060 TELEX 261580

RADIO SCRIPT

Date:	7 January 1986	Title:	They came from Outer Basingstoke
Client:	BRITISH RAIL	Length:	60 seconds
Product:	YOUNG PERSON'S RAILCARD	Word Count:	
SWO:		Submission No:	

Sound Effects   **Dialogue**

Burst of musical saw.

MVO: (1950s sci-fi voice, eg Twilight Zone)
It happened one March – all over the country young people were mysteriously being transported.

CINDY:
Disturbing news Greg – Now Chuck's gone.

GREG:
It's worse than that Cindy, so have Doug and Martha. You and I must be the only ones left.

CINDY:
Hey, have you noticed they're all between 16 and 23 years old?

Burst of music.

GREG:
I wouldn't mind betting there's an alien life-force behind all this.

Raging blizzard as door opens and shuts.

Cindy gasps.

GREG:
Kurt. Thank Heaven. You're a parapsychologist, what's going on?

KURT:
Speaking metaphysically, Greg, Cindy, diagnostic equation of an eight zero reduction percentage process confounding concession phenomena and existential eurphoria.

GREG:
Heck no! You mean they're getting up to 80% off Saver fares with a Young Persons Railcard this March.

KURT:
Ah huh!

CINDY: (accusingly)
Have you been communicating with the extraterrestrials Kurt?

KURT:
Kinda, Cindy. I went to the railway station and came back with this.

GREG:
A multi-faceted communication module?

KURT:
No Greg. A leaflet from stations or travel agents detailing amazing reductions for fun-loving young persons like ourselves.

MVO:
Be somewhere else with a Young Persons Railcard.

BRITISH RAIL/THE ARTIST

FACING PAGE Part of the original radio script.
BELOW Some of the artist's first lettering designs with the first couple.

Curiously his disappearance coincided with up to 80% off normal saver fare

Either the Martians have taken her or she's got a Young Persons Railcard.

Be somewhere else with a

With a Young Persons Railcard you can get huge reductions during March. Pick up a leaflet at your station or travel agent.

Disappear

Disappear with a ⇌ Young Persons Railcard

135

BRITISH RAIL/THE FINISHED VISUALS

GH What I normally do is make negatives from all the pictures and plan out the final image, then order all the prints to size and stick them all together.
DW Do you use spray mount or rubber solution (rubber cement)?
GH Spray mount. I cut them out first and make a montage, then have the whole thing re-photographed to get my master print, the one I actually tint up. This gets rid of all the joins and gives a flat surface to work on.
DW I notice that sometimes your style is different – the finished artwork looks a bit cruder. How do you get that effect?
GH By not bothering to re-photograph the first montage and working straight on it. But that wasn't right for this job.
DW Do you get the copy print done on any particular kind of paper?
GH I tend to have the final print done on Kentmere paper. It has a slightly rough texture, which interferes with the image a little, breaking it up a bit and making it look more like a drawing.
DW You can't 'knife' a highlight on textured paper though, as on ordinary bromide paper.
GH No, but I don't find that a problem, especially on a job like this where there's no need for really bright highlights.

ABOVE Geoff Halpin's finished visual with his original lettering and first young couple.
LEFT The replacement couple, thought to be of a more likely age to have teenage children.

BRITISH RAIL/THE FINISHED VISUALS

DW What inks do you use?
GH Mostly water-based airbrush inks and gouache for the opaque bits.
DW You've used gouache to do the halation around the disappearing figure, and I notice you've done it coarsely.
GH Yes, that's done with a splatter attachment on the airbrush.
DW It's not 'spot the deliberate mistake' then?
GH No! It just didn't work when it was smooth – it looked wrong. It had to be fairly gravelly to keep in style.
DW Was the halation done on an overlay?
GH It was on the rough, because at that stage we weren't quite sure how it was going to be done. But I did it on the surface on the actual artwork. In fact, everything was on the surface except the type. That was on an overlay because the copy kept changing.
DW It happens that way.
GH Well, that's the business. In fact the copy changed a couple of times after the ad was finished.
DW You designed a typeface for it originally, based on a fifties style. How did you arrive at that?
GH I was working on the fact that the job is a fifties pastiche, or parody maybe. I

ABOVE **The finished art before the type was added.**
FAR LEFT **The working print with the type in position.**
LEFT **The final image with British Rail's standard typeface replacing the artist's original typeface.**

137

BRITISH RAIL/THE FINAL IMAGE

looked at a lot of period typefaces in old type books, then did a slightly larger than life version of one – if you do these things accurately they just look old fashioned. You've got to exaggerate to make it more lifelike than it would have been at the time.
DW Did you hand draw all the little stuff as well?
GH I hand drew everything originally.
DW Going back to the actual tinting, how do you put the dyes on? Using an airbrush, or do you wash them on with a cotton ball?
GH I've never got into washing them on. I tend to use the airbrush.
DW Do you wet the print first?
GH Not normally. I sometimes wet it to mount it down – because photographic paper gets a bit wobbly sometimes.
DW Then you don't bother to dry mount?
GH No, I use rubber solution (rubber cement) or spray mount and if it's going to be laser scanned, I just tape it top and bottom.
DW Once you're ready to start colouring up, what do you use for masking? Adhesive film?
GH No, I use a moveable mask. I cut shapes out of acetate and move them slightly when I'm spraying. It gives a 'bad printing' effect which suits this style and is what I'm after.

ABOVE **The finished poster on site makes a strong impact.**
RIGHT **Press ads on the same theme were run in the national press.**

138

BRITISH RAIL/THE TECHNIQUES

1

2

Building colour: airbrush
1 Spray the image lightly to build up colour.
2 Be careful not to 'flood'.

1

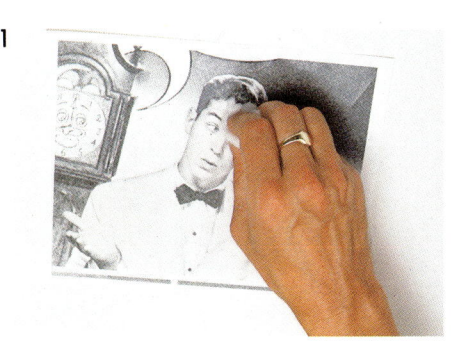

2

Building colour: dye
1 Using a cotton ball gently wash on the diluted dye.
2 Add more of the solution to build up to the desired tone.

1

Masking: drawing paper
1 Hold the mask in place with one hand and spray with the other.

2

2 A moveable mask gives a semi-soft line.

Experienced artists such as Geoff Halpin often break all the rules. The actual artwork is comparatively crude compared with other uses of the airbrush and other styles, but his methods are justified since the result is refreshingly spontaneous.

This kind of feeling can often be lost in the more polished types of illustration. Most artists who use photo-montage usually have the basic artwork re-photographed to disguise all the joins and give a flat surface to work on.

BUILDING UP COLOUR

Geoff Halpin uses the airbrush to colour the print. Such an experienced artist knows the strength of colour he has in his airbrush before it hits the paper, so he can be more confident than most. He uses dyes at full strength quite often as he knows their exact effect.

Airbrushing is more controllable than 'washing' the dye on using a cotton ball. This was the favourite method for hand-tinting photographs in the early part of the century and remained extremely popular until colour photography gradually took over. Dyes are diluted to a ratio of about two parts water to one part dye, depending on the strength of colour required. It is almost impossible to reduce colour once it is on the print so it's prudent to build the colour gradually until the desired tone is reached. Another problem is that the colours tend to spread. The print sometimes needs to be dry mounted to prevent 'cockling', or puckering.

MASKING

Using a 'moveable mask' to control the airbrushing gives a softer feel to the finished piece. It's possible to use clear acetate or even drawing paper for this purpose. The artist simply holds the mask in position with one hand and sprays round it. French curves can also be used to give a softer feel, while adhesive film masks give a harder edge.

The halation of the disappearing figure in the British Rail ad was sprayed directly on to the surface of the print last, using an acetate mask with a splatter-cap fitted on the airbrush. This was brave as it

139

BRITISH RAIL/PHOTO-MONTAGE

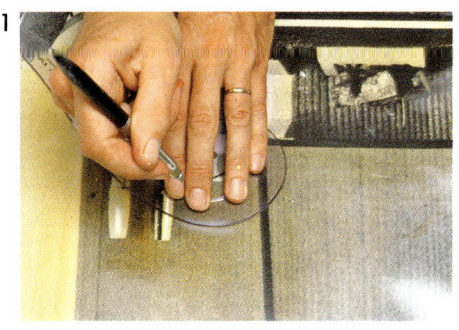

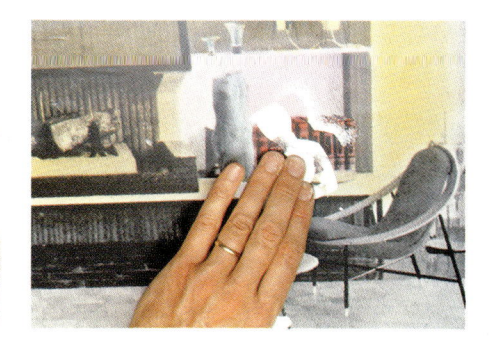

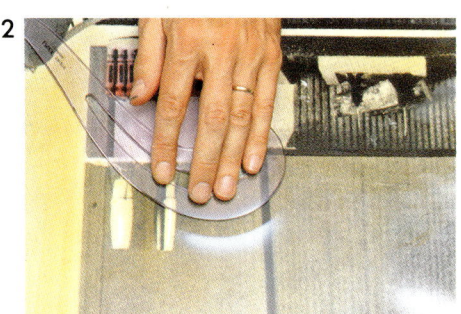

Masking: acetate
With the acetate mask in position spray on the halation using a splatter-cap fitted on the airbrush. Acetate gives a softer edge than adhesive film.

Masking: french curves
1 French curves can also be used to give a soft edge to the airbrushing.
2 Hold with one hand and spray with the other.

Masking: adhesive film
1 Stick the film over the print and cut round the desired area carefully.
2 Spray in the normal way.
3 The adhesive film mask gives a hard edge.

140

BRITISH RAIL/THE TECHNIQUES

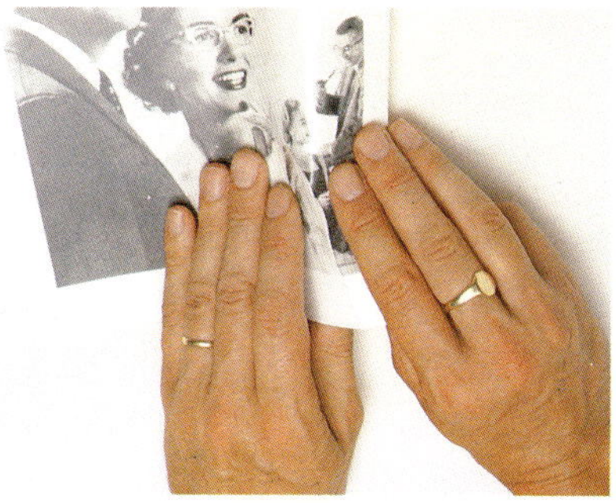

would have been impossible to alter if a mistake had been made. The artist could have sprayed the halation on an overlay, but this would have added to the reproduction costs.

STRIPPING

Sometimes it is necessary to strip the backing paper off the print to be montaged, to give an ultra thin edge. (This may save the need for recopying and the subsequent loss of quality.) The artist cuts lightly round the desired shape with a utility knife, making sure that it doesn't go through completely. Then, 'cracking' that line, the backing paper can be peeled away to leave the thinnest possible edge.

The white edge is then painted in a neutral tone. This is usually done after all the elements have been coloured separately.

HIGHLIGHTS

Sometimes hard highlights are required, in which case it is best to use ordinary bromide (glossy unglazed) paper, then a scalpel (utility knife) to 'knife' away the surface of the print to expose the whiteness underneath. An ordinary typist's eraser can be used in the same way to give a softer highlight.

Any solid colour that's required for highlights and so on is put on after the dye using gouache. The original then becomes more fragile, because gouache is water soluble and will wash off if more dye is added. For this reason, it's very important to finish all the tinting before adding gouache.

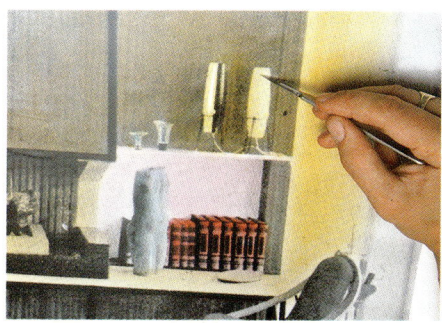

Highlights: knifing
1 Use a scalpel (utility knife) to 'scrape' the surface of the print.
2 Strong highlights can be created this way — but should be done after the tinting.

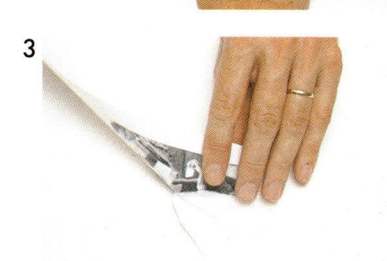

Stripping
1 Cut the required shape, taking care not to penetrate right through the base paper.
2,3 'Crack' the outside shape back and then peel off the backing paper carefully.

Highlights: soft
To achieve a soft highlight use a typist's eraser.
1 Rub quite hard. The surface of the print is gradually lightened.

141

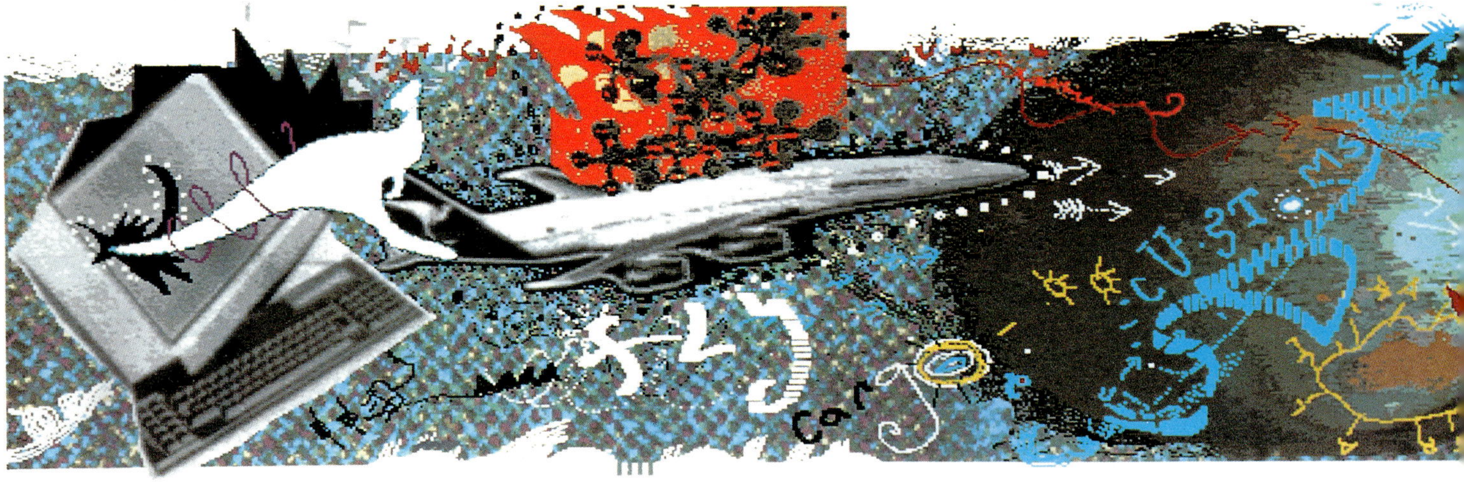
cargo
CUSTOMS

COMPUTER

Illustration by John England made on the Artron 2000 computer for Qantas.

The range and abilities of graphics computers continue to expand and the number of artists who are taking full advantage of them is growing too. One of the most useful aspects of these computers is their ability to do the more tedious work involved in the creation of an image. Laying a background can be done in seconds, and cutting a mask takes half the time it would if working conventionally — and the mask need only be cut once as the machine can hold it in it's memory. From here it can be recalled, and reversed, flipped and so on, all at the touch of a button.

The main problems associated with computer-generated material are in the output, which for reproduction purposes is in colour separations — transparencies are expensive to produce and prints are not of sufficient quality for reproduction. Also, the questions of copyright inherent in a system where the original is held on software that can be copied at will are a drawback.

COMPUTERS/THE FUTURE?

ARTIST DAVID NELSON
COMPUTER THE GRAPHIC PAINTBOX QUANTEL NEWBURY
THE BRIEF TO PRODUCE A COMMERCIALLY VIABLE ILLUSTRATION IN ONE DAY

In this age of advanced technology, it is possible to eliminate all the mechanical processes in the graphic arts. Unfortunately, faced with the technical complexities of the latest graphic computers, most artists simply do not know what to do. There seems to be a widespread lack of understanding and a general failure to utilize the capabilities of these extraordinary machines.

Although the computer can do whatever it is instructed to do, unless the job is a purely technical one such as retouching a transparency, the operator must be an artist. Drawing skills are as important here as they are for traditional work. Computer illustration is already becoming a specialized medium in its own right, but the speed and the almost infinite graphic abilities of the machine have scarcely been realized. All too often, artists are tempted to incorporate a bewildering array of graphic effects but without any design discipline.

However, even when the machines become cheaper and more accessible, and artists more skilful in their use, it seems unlikely that illustration as we

ABOVE David Nelson at work on the Quantel Paintbox.

RIGHT A proof produced directly from the computer using a sublimation transfer technique. Any image in the computer's memory can be printed instantly to this quality. Colour separations are printed out for finished art images.

QUANTEL
Graphic Paintbox

144

COMPUTERS/*THE FUTURE?*

COMPUTERS/THE FUTURE?

know it will become obsolete; a piece of artwork will always be more tangible than a strip of magnetic tape. No machine can achieve the immediacy and intimate involvement of the physical act of putting paint on paper, in whatever style. And, of course, there could be a 'backlash' against the use of computers as they become more widespread.

The foremost graphic computer is the Graphic Paintbox developed by the British company Quantel. The artist, David Nelson, had worked on the machine once, for a day, before he did this illustration, although he is familiar with computers. His brief was to produce a commercially viable illustration in one day, and he chose to do it in airbrush.

To save time, the tracing of the car was done in the normal way and then scanned into the computer before the artist started. It is possible to draw the trace straight on to the machine but, because David Nelson was not fully familiar with the Quantel Paintbox, it would have taken longer.

How a graphic computer works

The artist works on a hard desk-top pad using a stylus, all the time watching the image on the large upright screen in front of him or her. The options the computer offers are displayed on a 'menu', a changeable panel that normally appears on the bottom of the screen. To instruct the computer the artist simply presses the option wanted.

After the tracing has been drawn, a stencil (mask) is cut out; the brush size and 'medium' (that is, pencil, airbrush, and so on) can be selected, the stencil can be reversed, magnified and revised. Stencils are stored in the library, and can function whether or not they are displayed on screen.

The computer has two main drawing modes. The graphic mode is used to draw in straight lines and any graphic shape such as a circle, triangle and ellipse; all the artist does is select the shape, colour and brush thickness, and indicate the perimeters of the chosen shape with dots. In the painting mode, the artist chooses the method of applying colour – whether a paint stroke, a chalk line or airbrush, or a wash or tint – the size of the brush and the sharpness of the image. In both these modes, it is possible to call up the 'palette' from which any colours can be selected and mixed in whatever combination.

Using the pasteup mode, the artist can cut out an existing image and move it, or reduce or enlarge it. At every stage of the illustration, images can be banked in the library and then recalled when needed. The scanner mode is used to check through the images held in the file.

Cutting the stencil
This stencil (mask) is cut using the paintbrush, but any of the painting mediums can be used.
1 A transparency of a tracing of the car is scanned into the computer, using a Citex Scanner. It is possible to draw a tracing straight on to the computer, but in view of David Nelson's insufficient familiarity with the machine, this would have taken too long.
2 The artist selects a thin brush size to go round the image, which is then filled automatically. This basic stencil can also be reversed when it is time to do the background. At the top left of the image the original line crossed over itself, so the machine – which, after all, can't think for itself – fills to the outside shape of the red line.
3 The areas the machine missed are then magnified and touched up.
4 Then the stencil is enlarged so that the roof line can be sharpened.
5 The finished stencil with the menu shown.

COMPUTERS/*THE FUTURE?*

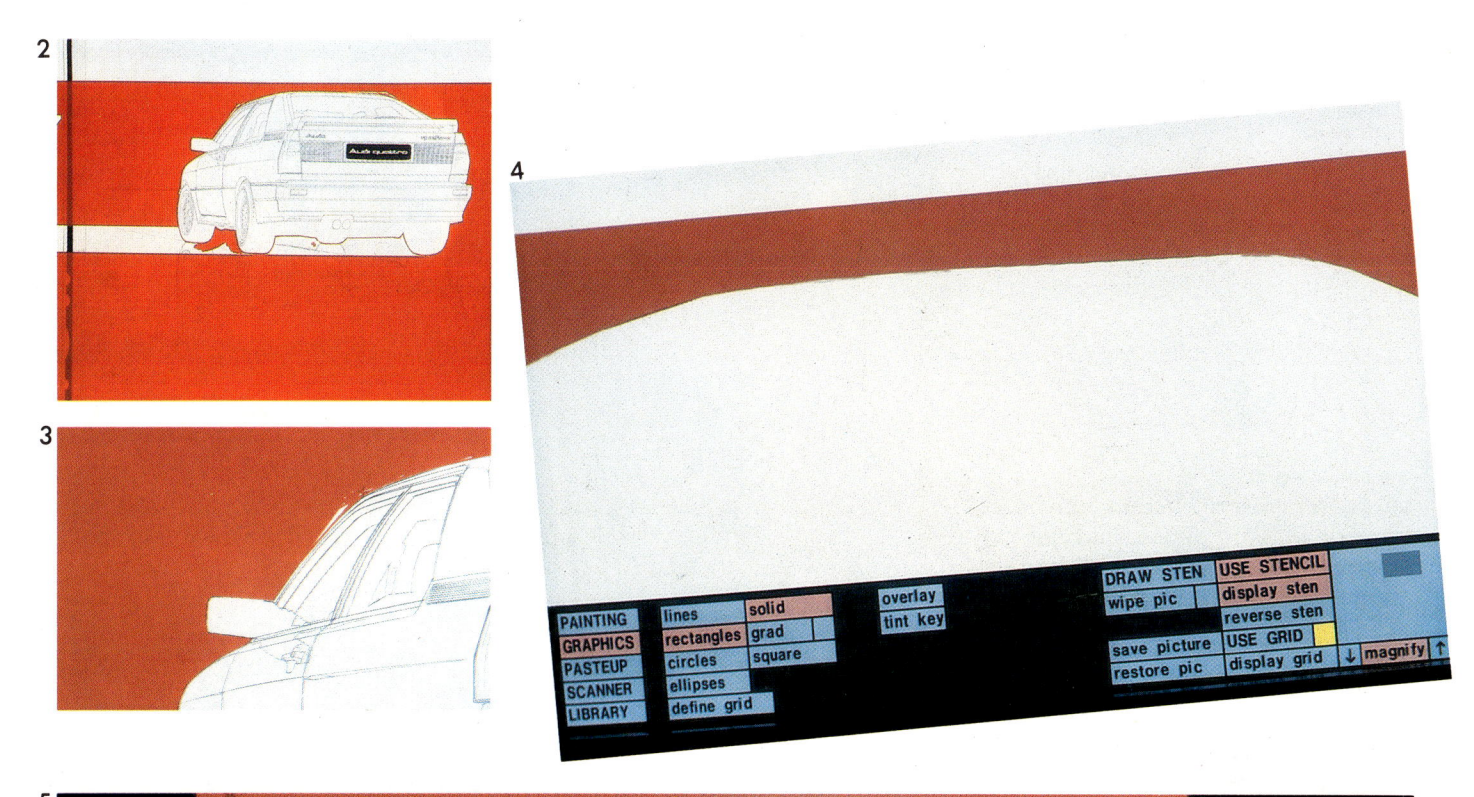

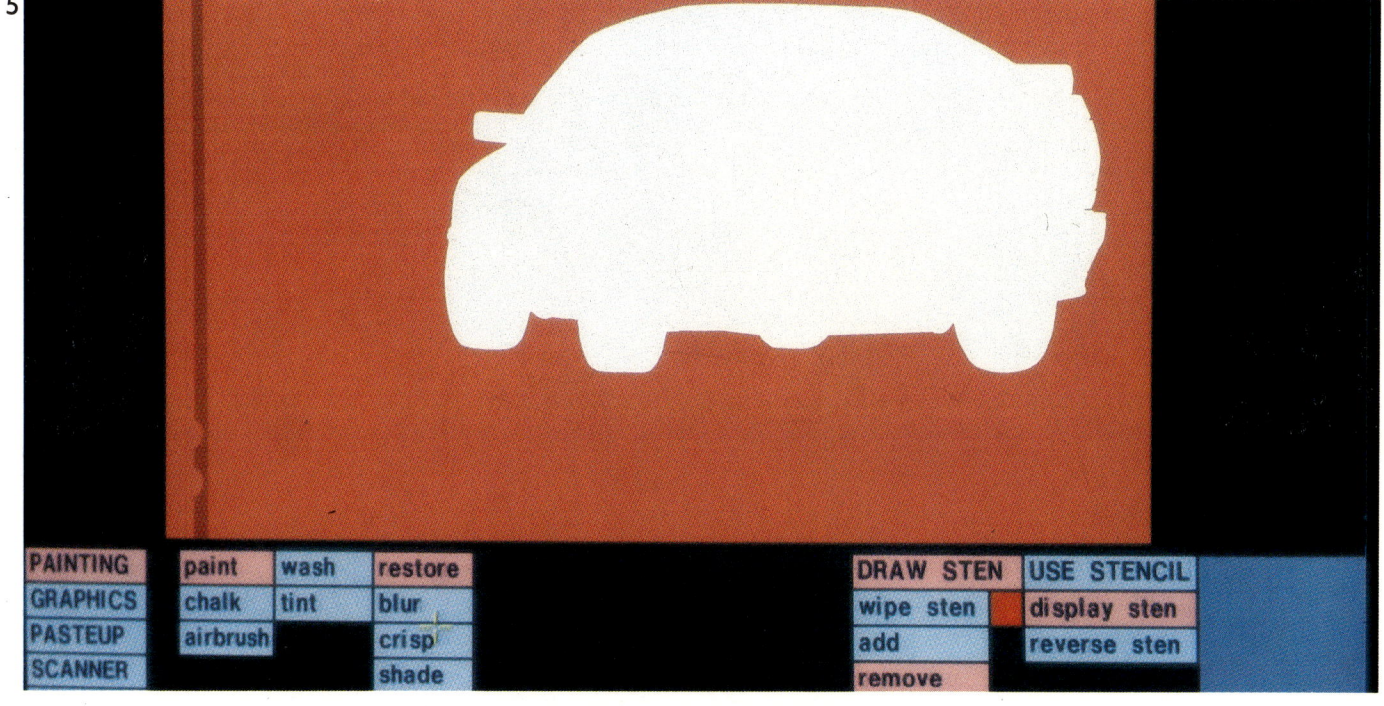

147

COMPUTERS /THE FUTURE?

148

COMPUTERS/THE FUTURE?

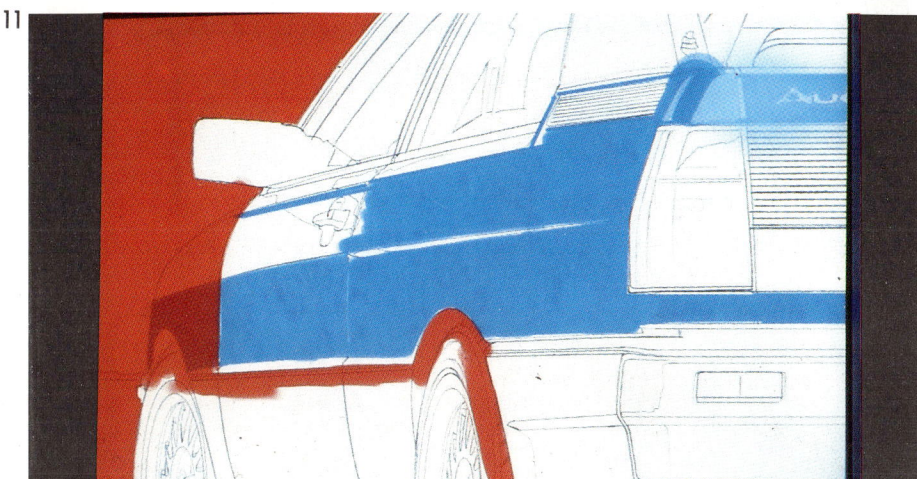

Painting lines
6 With the machine in graphic mode the first line is painted in blue. The stencil (mask) is on, but not displayed.
7 The palette with the range of colours to select from is shown at the bottom of the screen. The panel on the right selects the colour that is being used and the brush thickness. The straight lines are drawn in the same sequence as for a normal illustration. Here, the artist is starting to fill in the left-hand corner of the image with solid colour.
8 After enlarging the required section the artist can paint around the lettering without needing a stencil.

Airbrushing
9 The machine is now in airbrush mode. The menu at the bottom of the screen shows blue and white mixed on the palette. The artist has airbrushed the two together very softly so that he can sample some different shades. He then airbrushes the corner of the car to get a highlight. The stencil is on but not displayed.
10 Solid colour is being applied to the side of the car.
11 Towards the edges of the panels, which need to be lighter in colour, the artist starts to cut intermediate stencils. These can be cut and used, then held in the library for recall whenever needed. The main stencil can be seen here with an intermediate stencil around the doorline to define the edge of a different tone. The blues have been filled in down the side of the car and the highlight on the left-hand corner is finished.
12 The master stencil is in position and an intermediate stencil is being used while spraying a highlight back on to the door from the flared mudguard. Note the little green panel on the menu which indicates the airbrush strength or density.

149

COMPUTERS/THE FUTURE?

13 Another stencil (mask) has been cut to protect the highlight on the bottom of the door while the artist paints the shadow in solid blue.
14 Here, the stencil is taken a stage further. The highlight is masked around the lower half of the door, and a graduation is being sprayed down the lower shadow section.
15 The dark lower door is finished with the highlight retained. The menu is indicating that the machine is in airbrush mode, and using the stencil but not displaying it.

Painting in the details

16 To do the more intricate parts of the work — lots of reflections under the bumper, on the corners around the body mouldings, and the reflectors and lights set into it — the artist instructs the machine to magnify. He starts by filling in the reflections and will come back later in airbrush mode to soften them off. Different tones of blue are used, softened with lighter blues, all the time sampling from the different shades on the palette. An intermediate stencil for some of the intricate reflections on the bumper can be seen too.
17 A reversed stencil being made to cover most of the car.
18 The artist starts to airbrush a graduated tone across the bumper.
19 Making a stencil to mask all the areas that are not blue body colour, so the remaining body work can be airbrushed in.
20 To fill in the interior areas of the car and the blacks, the wheel arches and the tyres, the artist recalled the original trace with the original stencil from the library and combined it with another which had also been stored.

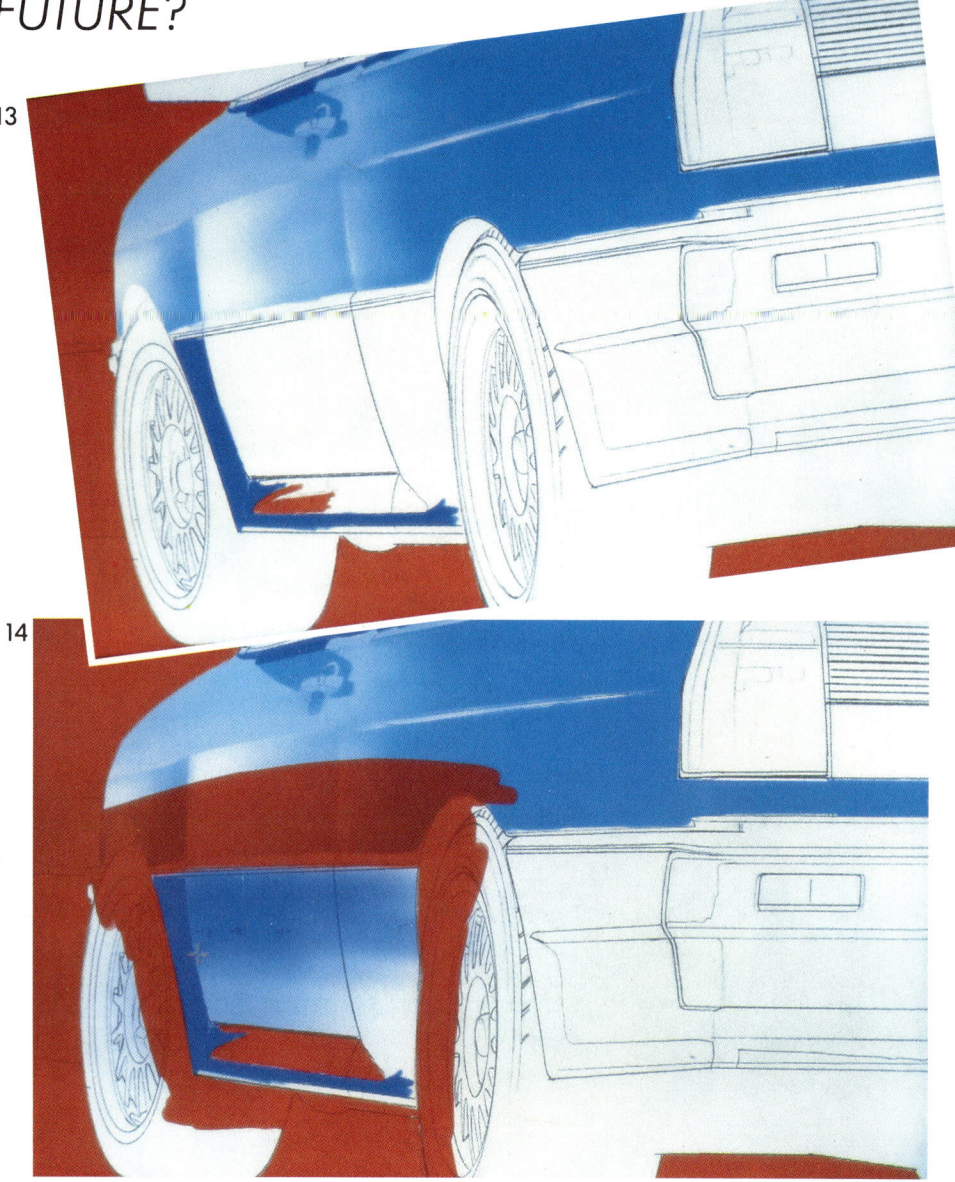

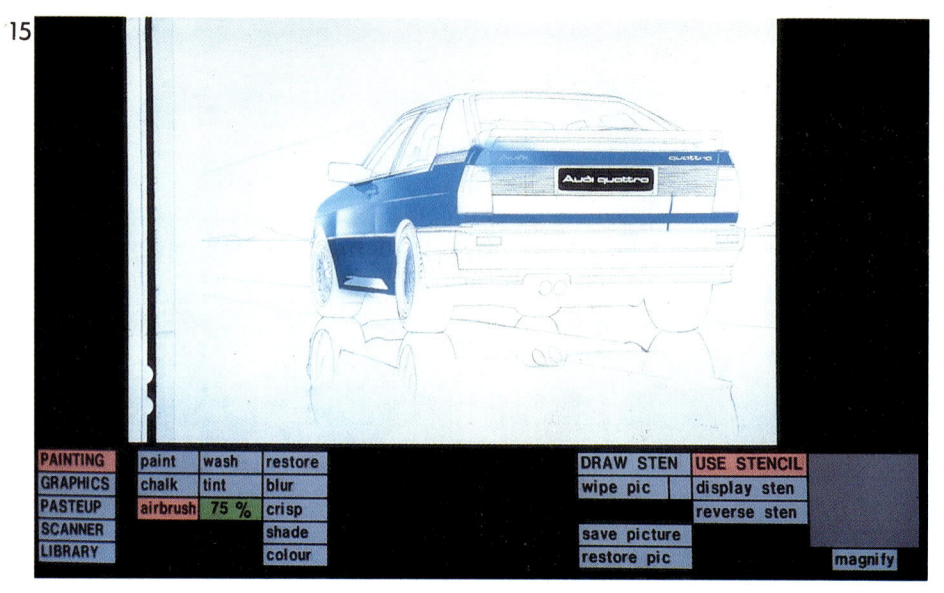

150

COMPUTERS/*THE FUTURE?*

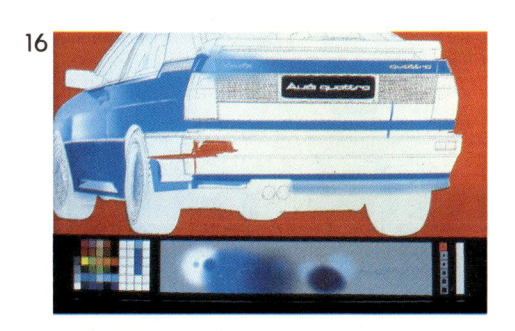

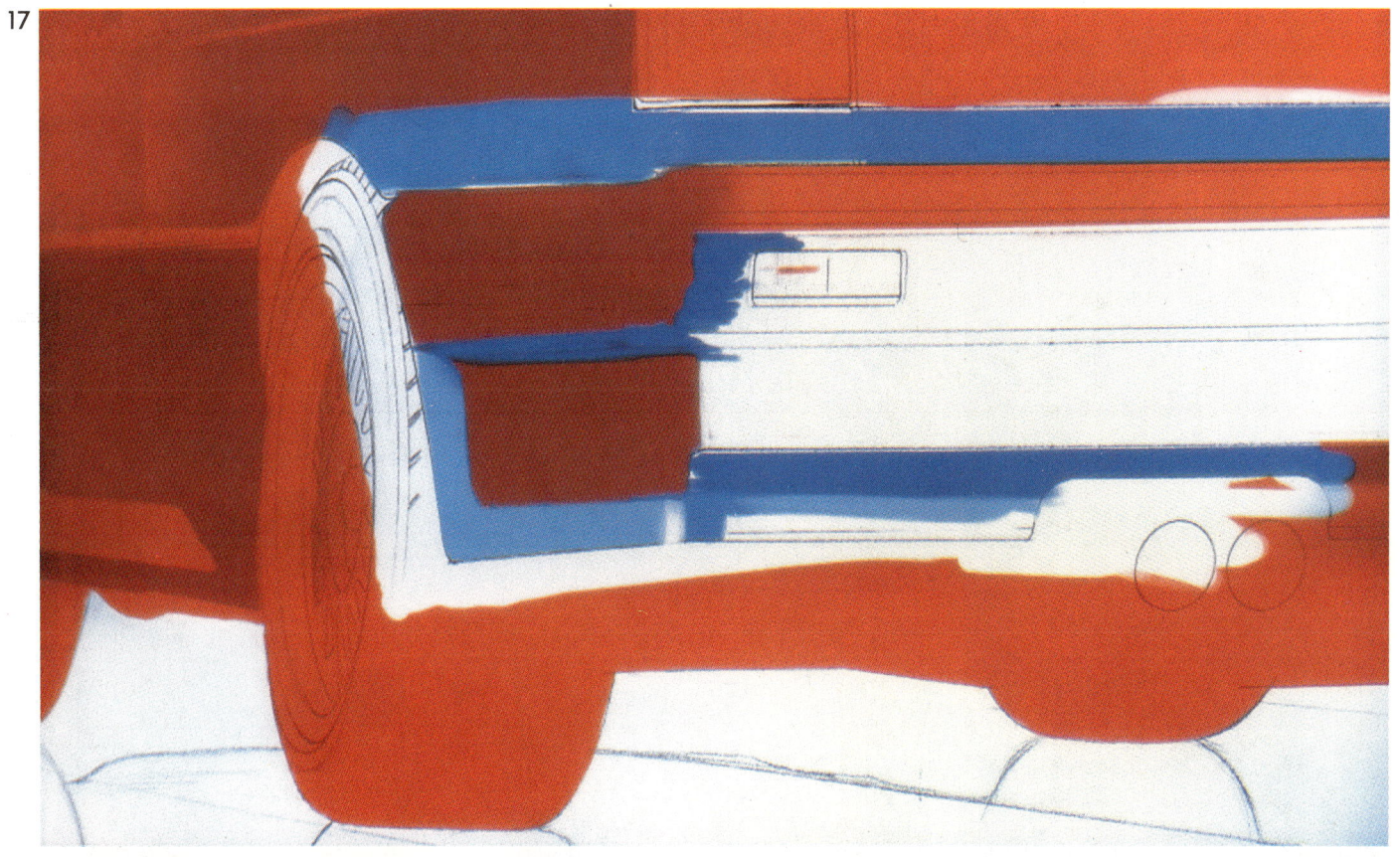

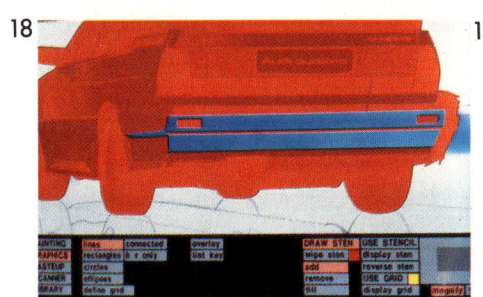

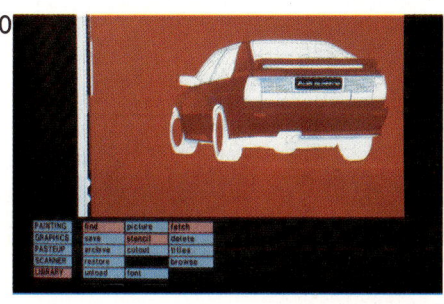

151

COMPUTERS/THE FUTURE?

152

COMPUTERS/THE FUTURE?

31

32

21 The new stencil, which is not shown on the screen, is placed on the work in progress, and the interior details airbrushed on over solid colour to give some depth.
22 The bodywork and the interior complete, the image is magnified in order to work on the small details such as the wing mirror and the door handle.
23 The stencils are shown in position, leaving the tyres, the underneath of the car and the panels, all of which are to be black, revealed. The artist is starting to fill in round the lettering.
24 The stencil is being used but not displayed, so the artist can match colours exactly. The palette at the top of the screen shows colours already used in the bottom part of the drawing.
25,26 To paint in the wheel the artist keeps changing from stencil displayed to not displayed in order to check exactly what is being covered and also to match the colour.

Drawing in the background
27 The shadow and a reflection on the ground are drawn in.
28 Using the graphic mode the artist draws a rectangle, and it fills in automatically, graduating from a light to dark colour selected from the blues on the palette in the left-hand corner.
29 The mountains are drawn in the painting mode with the stencil covering the car on but not revealed.
30 The horizon line was a guide only, and is airbrushed over. The mountain lines and reflection under the car are softened too.

Finishing the illustration
31 The finished blue car and background.
32 The cut-out car is saved in the library, then brought back and its colour blue is changed to red, using the tint function in the painting palette.

COMPUTERS /THE FUTURE?

33 The reflection is changed to red with the machine still in tint function, which will only colour tone and not black or white.
34 The stencil for the Audi symbol of interlocking circles is cut using the graphic mode.
35 The cut-out of the red car, which has been saved, is brought back and pasted over the new background.
36 The finished illustration: the symbol, and the red and blue cars have been brought back from the library, with a grey car made in the same way as the red one.

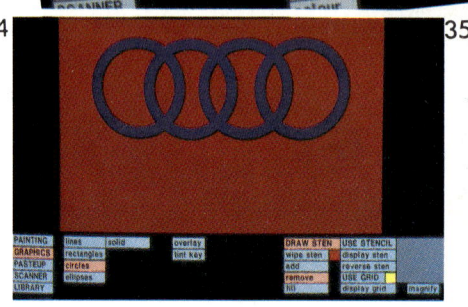

COMPUTERS/THE FUTURE?

It was appropriate that the Paintbox was used to produce these two ads for computer tapes.

Images like these can only be produced on a computer, and it remains to be seen whether advanced graphic technology will lead to computers becoming a medium in their own right or whether they will be used purely as a mechanical aid.

1 The artist was supplied with model shots of a heavily made-up man. The artist cuts through segments of the neck and then spaces them out, illustrating the gaps in between. Because it is possible to pick up not only exact colours but also textures, the skin texture is retained for the head and then the hair area is extended. The head distortion is achieved with the pasteup mode; a section is cut through and laid down slightly off angle. In fact the image can be distorted along an axis.

The background is made up of distorted copies of black-and-white architectural drawings; this is scanned into the computer and colour added on the tint mode. The airbrushed lines were added on graphic mode.

2 In this illustration, the background is made up of architectural drawings again — the airbrush lines are made in stencil and then reversed and tinted.

ACKNOWLEDGEMENTS

The author would like to thank Jenny Rodwell for her help with writing and Alan Jackson and Ian Sidaway for demonstration artwork.

PICTURE CREDITS

The author and the publishers would like to thank the following individuals and organizations for their permission to reproduce the illustrations in this book:

Advanced Business Concepts BV
Stadspoort 26
Postbus 2339
5600 CH
Eindhoven
(for Océ)

Paul Allen
Flat 4
36 Stanhope Road
Highgate
London
N6

The Artbox
Kruislaan 182
1098 SK
Amsterdam
(representing Geoff Nicholson and Ban Verkaek/Pem Sekeres)

Jensen Bolstead Reimers
Munkedamsvein 53b
0250 Oslo Z
(for BASF Tapes)

Anthony Brandt
73 New Bond Street
London
W1Y 9DD
(representing Larry)

Brunnings Advertising & Marketing
(Yorkshire Ltd)
Dudley House
Albion Street
Leeds
LS2 8PN
(for the Halifax Building Society)

CIA 36
36 Wellington Street
London
WC2E 7BD
(representing Murray Zanoni)

CM Spectrum Ltd
21–23 Meard Street
London
W1V 6PA
(for Dunlop)

Computer
Quantel
Kiln Road, Shaw
Newbury
Berkshire

Design Group
Happy Day Design
Weena 723
Postbus 29126
Rotterdam 3001 GC
(for Océ)

Collett Dickenson Pearce
110 Euston Road
London
NW1
(for Clan Tobacco)

DM B&B
2 St James's Square
London
SW1Y 4JN
(for Kleenex)

Folio
10 Gate Street
London
WC2
(representing Michael Bishop, Simon Fell, David Franklyn, John Harewood, Ann Sharp, George Underwood and Povl Webb)

Funny Business
61 Connaught Street
London
W2
(representing Ainslie MacLeod)

Geoff Halpin
25 Denmark Street
London
W1

Conny Jude
Flat 3
20 Steeles Road
London
NW3 4SH

Lintas
15–19 New Fetter Lane
London
EC4P 4EU
(for Barclays Bank)

Woodhams Lowe
76 Old Compton Street
London W1
(for Cherry 'B')

McCann-Industrieel
Kabelweg 21
1014 BA
Amsterdam
(for Borg-Warner Chemicals)

David Nelson
2 Hillside Terrace
Ascot Vale
Victoria 3032

Davidson Pearce
67 Brompton Road
London
SW3 1EF
(for the Dunkerque Tourist Board)

Saatchi & Saatchi Compton
80–84 Charlotte Street
London
W1 AQ
(for British Rail and Wines from Spain)

Lowe Howard Spink
Bowater House
114 Knightsbridge
London
SW1X 7LT
(for Bell's Whisky)

INDEX

Tavistock
59 Shelton Street
London
WC2 9HE
(for Angostura Bitters)

TBWA
27 Floral Street
London
WC2E 9DQ
(for Evian)

Thorogood Burgess
5 Dryden Street
London
WC2E 9NW
(representing Peter Blandemer and Tony Gilliam)

Top Drawers
Entrepotdok 67 & 77A
10018 AD
Amsterdam
(representing Marcel Rozenburg)

Virgil Pomfret
25 Sispara Gardens
London
SW18 1LG
(representing Tom Adams)

Waldron Allen Henry & Thompson
100 Brompton Road
London
SW3 1EK
(for Commercial Union Insurance)

White Collins Rutherford Scott
44 Great Queen Street
London
WC2B 5AR
(for Qantas)

Yellowhammer
46 Wigmore Street
London
W1H 9DF
(for Ward White)

Young Artists
2 Greenland Place
London
NW1
(representing Amy Burch)

page numbers in bold contain illustrations

Acetate masks 139, **140**
Acrylics 32–3, **33**–**55**
   airbrush 15–16, 18, **18–21**, 33, 53
   on wood 51–4, **51**, **53**, **54–5**
   technique 41–2, **42–3**, 44, **44–5**, 46, **46–7**, 51–4
Adams, Tom 34, **36–47**
   finished images **34–5**, **39**, **40–1**
   references **37**, **38**
   technique 38, **39**, 41–2, **42–3**, 44, **44–5**, 46, **46–7**
Adhesive masking film 13, **18–19**, **20–1**, 26, **27**, 28–30
   dot film 21
   fluid 71, **71**
   sprays 96
Agencies,
   Advanced Business Concepts 48
   Davidson Pearce 88
   DMB & B 98
   Lintas 10
   Lowe Howard Spink 34
   McCanns Industrieel 22
   Saatchi & Saatchi 74, 132
   Tavistock 122
   TBWA 58
   Yellowhammer 110
Airbrushing 8, **9–31**, 53, **54**
   computer **149–153**
   photo-montage 137, **138**, 13, **140**
   techniques 13, **14**, 15–16, 18, **18–19**, **20–1**, 25–7, **26–7**, **28–30**
Allen, Paul 10–21
   finished images **11**, **12**
   technique 13, **14**, 15–16, 18, **18–19**, **20–1**
   traces 13, **14**, 15
Architecture
   airbrush 26, **26**, **27**, 30
   computer **155**
   line & wash 80, **81**, 81, **82**, 82, **83**
   pencil **97**

Art directors
   R. Berckenkamp 22, 24–5, **24–5**
   L. Cash 132, **133**, 133–4
   R. Cazemage 74, 76, 77, **77**, 79
   D. Christensen 34–6, **34**
   B. Connolly 10, **10**, 12, **12**, 15
   M. Engelaan 48, 50, **50**
   M. Gaskin 58, 60
   J. Hodges 98, **99**, 100–1
   J. Knight 58–60, **60**
   L. Loef 48, 50–1, **50**
   P. Lynch 88, **88**, 90–1
   R. Nash 122–4, **126**
   J. Pemberton 110, **110**, 112–13
Art education 124
Artists
   T. Adams 34, 36–47
   P. Allen 10–21
   M. Bishop 88–97
   P. Blandemer 110–19
   A. Burch 98–107
   G. Halpin 132–41
   C. Jude 58–71
   Larry 122–9
   D. Nelson **144**– 55
   G. Nicholson 22–31
   M. Rozenburg 48–55
   M. Zanoni 74–85

Backgrounds,
   acrylic 51, 53, 54, **54**
   airbrush 15, **20–1**, 28
   computer 143, 146, **147**, **153**, **155**
Berckenkamp, Dick 22, 24–5, **24–5**
Berry, Graham 35
Bishop, Michael 88–97
   finished images **89**, **93**, **94**, **95**, **97**
   proofs **91**
   technique 92–3, **92–3**, 96, **96–7**
   working traces **90**, **94**, **95**
Blandemer, Peter 110–19, **110**
   finished images **111**, **115**
   technique 112–14, **112–14**, 115–16, **116–17**, 118, **118**, **119**
   traces **112**, **113**, **114**
Bleaching 63

157

Boards
    line 18, 25, 68, **68**
    scraperboard 109, 113, 115–16
Bockingford paper 65, 68, **68**
Browne, Chris 74, 76–7
Brush & rule technique 71, **71**
Brushes
    acrylics 42, 45, 46, 53, 55
    computer 146
    scraperboard 116, 117, 118
    touching-up 26
    watercolour 69
Burch, Amy 98–107
    finished images **98**, 99
    references 100–1
    technique 102, **102**, 103–4, **103**, **104**, 105–7
Burnishing 21

Campaign briefs
    Angostura 122–3
    Barclays Bank 10, 12
    Bell 34–6
    Borg Warner 22, 24
    British Rail 132–4
    computers 142
    Dunkerque 88, 90–2
    Evian 58–60
    Kleenex 98, 100–1
    Océ 48, 50
    Spanish wines 74, 76, 79
    Ward White 110, 112–13
Cars
    airbrush 26, 27
    computer 144–54
    scraperboard **118**
Cartoons 120–1, 121–9
    technique 124–6, **126**, 128–9
Cash, Linda 132, **133**, 133–4
Cazemage, Roger 74, 76, 77, **77**, 79
Christensen, D. 34–6, **34**
Computers, graphics 142–3, 143–55
    proofs **145**, **154**, **155**
    technique 146, **146–54**
Connolly, Brian 10, **10**, 12, **12**, 15
Copy lines
    Angostura 123, 124
    Barclays 17

    B. Rail **135**, 137
    Dunkerque 88, **89**, **95**
    Evian 58–9, 60
    Océ 48, 50
    Spanish wines 79
Copyscanners (Camera Lucida) 13, 63, 65, 66, 101, 102
Copywriters
    C. Browne 74, 76–7
    T. de Silva 88, 88–9, 90–2
    J. Eley 10
    R. Mol 48
    L. Murrell 132, 133–4
    A. Page 110
    H. Van Wel 22
Crayons, use 61, 65

Daler line board 68, **68**
Design group, Happy Day 48, **49**
Dip pens 84, 118
Dot film 21
Drafting machine, scraperboard 116, 117, 118
Draw-film 21
Drawing size 64, 66
Drawing technique 124

Engelaan, Martin 48, 50, **50**
Engraving, scraperboard 117, 118
Epidioscope 38
Erasers, typist's 9, 16, 18, 26, 27, 141, **141**

Fixative spray 96
Flesh tones
    airbrush 16, 18, **18–19**
    pencil drawings 103
    scraperboard 119
    watercolours **70**
Franklyn, David 72–3
French curves 26, 139, **140**

Gaskin, Malcolm 58, 60
Gilliam, Tony 108–9
Glass, reflections 44–5, **44–5**
Gouache,
    airbrush 25, 26, 27, 30
    pencil drawings 92, 96
    photo-montage 141

    watercolours 63, 80
Graphic devices 12, **12**, 14, 16, 20–1, **21**
Grass, scraperboard **118**

Hairdryers 28
Halation 139–40
Halpin, Geoff 132–41
    finished images **132**, **136**, **137**, **138**
    lettering **135**, 136
    technique 136–7, **137**, **138**, 139, **139**, **140**, 141, **141**
Hand painting 20, 38–47
Hands
    airbrush 13, 16, **18–20**
    scraperboard **119**
Harewood, John 8–9
Heads, computer **155**
Heat effects 53, 126
Highlights
    acrylic 41, **44**, **45**, 46, **46–7**
    airbrush 9, 16, 18, 25–6, **27**, **29**, **30**
    computer **149**, **150**
    glass 44, **45**
    pencil 92, 96
    photo-montage 136, 141, **141**
    scraperboard 117, **118**
    watercolours **70**
Hodges, Jo 98, **99**, 100–1

Ink drawings, cartoons 122–9
Inks
    airbrush 15–16, 18, 25, 26–7
    Indian 126
    photo-montage 136
    scraperboard 116, 117
    water-based 63, 137
    waterproof 25, 26–7, 84, **84**, **85**

Jude, Conny 58–71
    finished images **58–9**, **61**, **62**, **64**, **66**
    technique 62, 63, 65, **65**, 66, **66**, 67, **67**, 68–71, **68–71**
    working traces **62–3**

158

Kentmere paper 136, 138
Kitchen, Rob 132, 133
Knight, John 58–60, **60**

Larry 122–9
   finished images **122–3,**
      125–7, 129
   technique 124–6, **126, 128,** 129
Laying a wash 69, **69,** 79–80,
   82–3, 85
Lettering 135
   by hand 20, 41
   watercolours 71, **78**
Light box 62–3, 70
Line & wash 72–3, 72–85
   finished images **72–3, 74,**
      75, 76, 78, 80, 82, 83
   techniques 79–82, **82, 83,**
      84, **84,** 85
Line board 24, 68, **68**
Lines, ruling 27, **43,** 44, 51, 71, **71**
Loef, Leen 48, 50–1, **50**
Logos 48, **79,** 79, 91
Lynch, Paul 88, **88,** 90–1

Macleod, Ainslie **120–1**
Mahogany, colours 42–3, **42–3**
Mahogany support 52, 53, 54, **54**
Masking 26–7, 28–30, 53, 54
   airbrush 13, 14, 18, **18,** 19,
      20–1, 138, 139, **139,** 140
   computer 143, 146, **146–54**
   photo-montage 138, 139,
      139, 140
   watercolours 65, 71, **71**
Masking film 13, 18–19, 20–1,
   26, 27, 28–30, 140
   dot 21
Masking fluid 71, **71**
Masking sprays 96
Masks, moveable 21, 138, 139, **139**
Menu, computer 146–7
Metals
   acrylic 46, **46–7**
   see also cars
Models 37, **38,** 65
Mounting 38, 41, 116
   spray 136, 138
Movement effects 52, **53,** 54, 63

Murrell, Lorna 132, 133, **133,** 134

Nash, Robin 122–4, **126**
Nelson, David 144–55
   proofs **145, 154, 155**
   stencils (masks) 146, **146–54**
   technique 146, **146–54**
Nicholson, Geoff 22–31
   finished images **22–3,** 31
   technique 25–7, **26–7, 28–30**

Optical mixing 103, **105–6**
Overlaying 103, **105**

Painting by hand 9, 16, 20,
   38–47, 53
Palette, computer 146, **148,**
   149, **153**
Paper
   Bockingford 65, 68, **68**
   cartridge 38, 41, 106
   coloured 106
   layout 127
   mounting 38, 80
   pencil drawings 92, 96, 102
   photographic 136, 138
   Saunders 68, **68,** 80
   stretching **84**
   tracing 63, 113
   typing 126, 127
   watercolours 65, 68, **68,** 80
   Waterford 68, **68,** 92
   Whatman 68, **68**
Pemberton, Jeremy 110, **110,**
   112–13
Pen & ink 79, 84
Pencil drawings 38, **86–7,**
   87–107, 121, 124
   technique 92–3, **92–3,** 96, **96–7**
Pencils
   coloured 87, 103–4, **104,**
      105, 106, **107**
   pastel 113, 116
   watersoluble 87, 106, **107**
   white 96, 113, 116
   with acrylics 38
   with watercolours 57, 63, 70
Pens
   cartoons 121, 126

line & wash 73
mapping 73, 126
scraperboard 118
technical 73, **117,** 118, 126
Perspectives, buildings 27, 80,
   81, 82
Photocopies as masking 26, 27,
   28–9
Photocopying 26
Photographic paper 136, 138
Photographs advertising 12,
   24, 36, 51, 98, 100, 113,
   123–4, 131
Photographs as references
   acrylics 36, **38,** 51, 54
   airbrush **13,** 15, 26
   line & wash 79, 80–2
   pencil 90, 100–1, 101–2
   scraperboard 118
   watercolours 65, **66**
Photo-montage **130–1,** 131–41
   technique 136–7, **137,** 138,
      138, 139, **139,** 140, 141, **141**
Pigments
   acrylics 33
   watercolours 57
Putty rubber, for lightening 92, 96

Quantel graphic paintbox **144–55**

Radio script 132, 133, 134, **134**
Rapidographs (technical pen)
   73, **117,** 118, 126
References 36, 37, **37,** 52, 65–6
   photographs see photographs,
      references
Reflections
   glass 44–5, **44–5**
   metal 46, **46–7**
   see also cars
Retarders 53
Retouching varnish 38, 41, 43,
   44, **45,** 45–7
Rozenburg, Marcel 48–55
   finished images 48, **49,** 52–3
   technique 51–4, **51, 53, 54–5**
Ruling lines 27, **43,** 44, 51, 71, **71**

Saunders paper 68, **68**, 80
Scalpels, for highlights 9, 16, 26, 27, **29**, 141, **141**
Scanner, Citex **146**
Scraperboard 108–9, 109–19
   technique 112–14, **112–14**, 115–16, **116–17**, 118, **118**, **119**
Scrapers **114**, **117**, 118
Sharpe, Anne 32–3
Sketches, as references 65–6, 79, 81
Skies
   airbrush 53
   scraperboard **93**, 118
Skin
   airbrush 18–19
   computer **155**
   scraperboard 119
Smudging 93, 96
Splatter caps 93, **93**, 137, **139**
Sponges 69
Stencils, computer 146, **146–54**
Stripping, photo-montage 141, **141**
Sublimation transfer technique 144–55
Supports **see** boards, paper, wood

Television 74, 98, **100**
Templates for masking 26, **29**
Textures
   acrylic 42, **42–3**, 44, **44–5**, 46, **46–7**, 54
   pencil drawing 96, **96–7**
   scraperboard 118, **118**, **119**
   watercolours **70**
Tinting, computer 153–4
Toning
   airbrush 16, 18–19, 139
   computer **149**, **150–1**
   pencil drawing 92, 96, **96–7**, 104
   scraperboard 116–17
   watercolours 70, **70**
Touching up, airbrush 16, 26
Touching-up, pencil 92
Traces 13, 26
   computer 146
   lettering **78**

pencil drawing 94–5, **102**
scraperboard **112**, 113, **113**, 116
watercolours 61, **62**, 63, **63**
Trompe l'oeil 35, 36
Typefaces **135**, 136–7, **138**
Typing paper 126

Underwood, George, pencil 86–7

Varnishing 38, 41, 43, **43**, 45, **47**, 53

Washes, application 69, **69**, 82–5
Watches, airbrush 27, 28–9
Watercolours 56–7, 56–71
   laying a wash 69, **69**
   line & wash 72–3, **73**, 79–80, 84
   techniques 62, 63, 65, **65**, 66, 67, **67**, 68, **68**, 70, **70**, 71, **71**
Waterford paper 68, **68**, 92
Waterproof inks 25, 26–7, 84, **84**, 85
Webb, Paul, watercolours 56–7
Whatman paper 68, **68**, 92
White paint, highlighting 16, 18
Wood, as support 52, **54**
Wood grain
   acrylics 42, **42–3**
   scraperboard 118
Working traces
   acrylics 26–27
   line & wash 80
   scraperboard 112–13
   watercolour 61, **62–3**

Zanoni, Murray 74–85
   finished images 74, **75**, **76**, **80**, **82**, **83**
   technique 79–82, **81**, 83, **84**, **84**, 85
   traces **80**

NC
1000   Ward, Dick
.W37
1988   Creative ad de-
        sign & illustra-
        tion

DUE DATE